CAREGIVING INSIGHTS

WISH I KNEW SERIES

CAREGIVING INSIGHTS

WISH I KNEW SERIES

LISE LEBLANC

Wish I Knew: Caregiving Insights

Editor: Allister Thompson

Book Designer: Jamie Arts

Published in Stratford, Canada, by Blue Moon Publishers.
Printed and bound in Canada.

ISBN: 978-1-988279-93-0

Next Chapter books are available at special quantity
discounts to corporations, professional associations and
other organizations. For details and discount information,
please contact marketing@bluemoonpublishers.com.

CONTENTS

ABOUT THE WISH I KNEW CAREGIVER COLLECTION

The Wish I Knew Caregiver Set offers something for every caregiver, whatever stage they are at. Arranged in brief sections, they can be consumed during your caregiving journey, if you only have time to read in a waiting room, while warming up lunch, or during your loved one's nap.

The *Conscious Caregiving Guide* focuses on conscious caregiving and self-care, with brief sections that are broken down with tips, practical exercises, reflective questions, and real-life examples.

The *Conscious Caregiving Guide Workbook* is your essential workbook to accompany the *Conscious Caregiving Guide*. Each chapter in the workbook corresponds to a chapter in the book, including practical exercises, checklists, reflective questions, and more.

Caregiving Insights offers brief stories that offer unique perspectives on caregiving.

Gentle Quotes on Caregiving are brief passages for the harried caregiver who may only have time for a line or two.

The *Caregiving Guided Journal* offers a chance to reflect, recharge, and set aside time for your own self-care.

FOREWORD

Every family has a caregiving story... for better or worse, for richer or poorer, in sickness and in health. Most couples have used just these words as marriage vows promising to provide comfort and care for, "as long as they both shall live."

I'd venture to say, however, that during those tender moments in front of friends and family, neither party gave much thought to what I like to refer to as their "caregiving years." They likely have not discussed how changing circumstances over the years would affect their relationship, their quality of life, their financial situation, their home life and the help they'd have to give or receive.

And can you blame them? Even for those who are not the marrying sort, the topics of retirement planning and financial matters, along with dreams of living somewhere warm, carefree, and affordable usually carry these types of conversations.

Truth is, life happens. Families also drift or fall apart, come back together, blend, change, and grow. Some thrive. Some don't. Regardless, somewhere in our mid to late forties, reality comes knocking for most of us. There's a sibling, a child, a parent, or maybe even a spouse who needs help. And, perhaps, a lot of it. The facts speak for themselves:

> More than 8 million Canadians provided informal care to a family member or friend.[1]
> More than 1 million caregivers are older than 65.[2]
> 44% of caregivers between the ages of 45–64 care for both a parent and children.[3]
> The number of seniors requiring care is set to double over the next 15 years.[4]
> 39% of caregivers look after the needs of their parents; 8% care for a spouse.[5]
> 35% of Canada's workforce provides informal, unpaid care while working.[6]
> 1.6 million caregivers take time off work to provide care.[7]
> One-in-ten caregivers spends more than 30 hours per week providing care.[8]

Caregiving, if we choose to take it on, (and it is a choice), can be a labour of love or a duty depending on who you are. It can be offered hands-on or from afar. It can be full or part time, for a short time or for years. It's a journey through paths unknown that can push a person to their limits and bring out the best or worst in current and past relationships. And no doubt, it's difficult when working, raising a family, going through personal relationship challenges, or raising a child who needs a great deal of extra attention. Yes, looking after someone else can be fraught with financial challenges, emotions, hope, and disappointment. Those who have walked before us will attest to the fact that assuming the role of "carer" it's often referred to these days, is filled with moments of tenderness, kindness, awkwardness, and unfortunately frustration and tribulation.

But, for better or worse, caregiving is simply part of everyday family life for most of us, sooner or later. So, explore the wonderful stories and lessons learned that are shared by experts and laypeople in this book, all with lived experience. I wish you peace, joy, and most of all, increased awareness that will make the time you spend looking after a loved one as stress free, effective, and rewarding as possible for as long as you shall live.

Caroline-Tapp MacDougall
Founder of Canada Cares
Development Manager of Canadian Abilities Foundation

REFERENCES:

1. Statistics Canada. 2012. "Portrait of Caregivers."
2. Report from the Employer Panel of Caregivers. 2015. "When Work and Caregiving Collide."
3. Ibid.
4. Ibid.
5. Statistics Canada. 2012. "Portrait of Caregivers."
6. Report from the Employer Panel of Caregivers. 2015. "When Work and Caregiving Collide."
7. Ibid.
8. Ibid.

EDITOR'S NOTE

When my publisher asked me to create a collection book on caregiving to accompany the *Conscious Caregiver's Guide*, I said: *Sure, no problem!* I'd been a caregiver both personally and professionally and had learned a lot about what to do (and not do) as a caregiver, but I was very eager to hear about other people's caregiving experiences and the lessons they'd learned. *I* had no clue how deeply I would be impacted by the compassionate, vulnerable, "in the trenches" stories shared by these inspirational authors. At times I was bawling, other times I was laughing out loud. Most of the time I found myself connecting with the raw mix of authentic emotions as I easily identified with the profound personal admissions, struggles, triumphs, rewards, fears, and challenges they all faced along their caregiving journeys. What struck me most were the unique perspectives and powerful lessons contained in each story. I had so many ah-ha moments, and I am quite confident you will too. As you will discover, these stories are deeply personal and profoundly impactful. They will help you view your caregiving experience in a whole new light by giving you the awareness, insight, and inspiration to be a more conscious caregiver.

—Lise Leblanc

CHAPTER ONE

LIFE ON THE RECEIVING END

LINA MIRANDA

Knowing life on the other side of caregiving, or anything else, is impossible, but Lina Miranda bravely shares insights of what it was like for her after her cancer diagnosis at the age of twenty-one. The wishes and hopes of a person during this stricken stage may not be possible, but learning from Lina is.

People often say it's those left behind by the loss of a loved one who suffer the most. While there is truth in this belief, caregivers can suffer intensely while taking care of a loved one. The strain a caregiver endures — emotionally, physically, and mentally — is heavy and consuming. Being a caregiver can be a tremendously difficult role. As a caregiver, you may be left questioning whether you are doing too much or too little. Are you talking too much? Not listening enough? Asking too many questions? Hovering? Not present enough? Having to adapt to the mood or needs of the care recipient from day to day can, at times, feel like watching the ball at a roulette table; you never know where it's going to land. Taking on this role, or in some cases being forced into this role, is like stepping onto a rollercoaster ride with inevitable ups and downs. Feelings of anger, frustration, exhaustion, and hopelessness are common and to be expected. I would imagine that many caregivers at times throughout their journeys feel like they are walking on eggshells, always trying to be exactly what their loved one needs without being able to express their own feelings out of fear of upsetting their care recipient.

I have been on the other side of the equation. Having been a care recipient, I can provide perspective on how to best be a caregiver through the lens of a care receiver, in my case, as a cancer patient. There were a number of things that my caregivers did well and for which I will forever be grateful. But there were also things I wish they'd done differently. There are two things in particular I really wish my caregivers had done that none of them did. I didn't know at the time that I needed these two things, but now, eighteen years later, after years of thought, I realize they are essential for all caregiving situations.

My journey as a care recipient started at a time in my life when my best friend and I were planning a backpacking trip. I was twenty-one, getting ready to go on this amazing trip to spend the summer in Europe with my friend, when one day my dad said, "Lina this doctor keeps calling for you."

I thought, *That's strange, but if he's not leaving a message, it mustn't be that important. He'll just have to catch me when I get back!* A few days later, I was home when he called. I picked up the phone, and the first thing he said to me was, "Lina are you sitting down?" I remember thinking, *This is not good.* He said, "We found a tumour. It's big, and we will need to work fast." As I hung up the phone, I just sat on my bed looking at my backpack, thinking, *This is serious. Not only am I not going to Europe, but I might die.*

My symptoms started when I was eighteen. I was in my first year of university when I told my family physician about my heartburn. He chalked it up to anxiety and said it was fairly typical for new students. But as the year went on, my symptoms became more of a constant, rather than episodic pain. In follow-up visits, he continued to insist that my pain was stress-induced. A few months after another unsuccessful visit with my doctor, I ended up in the emergency room with severe heartburn that took my breath away. It felt as though someone had poured gasoline down my throat and lit a match in my stomach. At the ER, I was given morphine for my pain and after a night of observation was sent home. It was after this ER visit that my family doctor thought there was potentially something else going on other than stress. I was tested for *H. pylori*, bacteria that causes stomach ulcers. Not surprisingly, I tested positive for the bacteria and was put on an antibiotic regime to treat it.

Unfortunately, as time went by, my symptoms worsened. I ended up back in ER a few months after my first visit. I was again given morphine by intravenous for the pain, observed overnight, and then discharged the next morning.

After almost two years of suffering from severe and almost constant heartburn, I decided to take matters into my own hands and do some research. My investigation led me to request a scope of my stomach. My doctor thought I was being overly concerned but agreed to follow my wishes and put me on a waiting list for a gastrointestinal scope. However, due to my young age, it would be a long wait. Many painful days and nights went by, and once again I ended up back at the ER. I was embarrassed by the fact that it was my third time to the ER with the same symptoms. But this particular visit was different; the ER doctor was concerned by my frequent visits and worried I might have a perforated ulcer. It was the only explanation he could think of for the extreme pain. He admitted me as an inpatient so I could have my scope done the next day. The following morning, I met the gastroenterologist, who asked me if I drank a lot of cola or took a lot of ibuprofen, or if I had noticed any blood in my stool — a resounding no to all. I sensed his hesitation to do the scope, but thankfully, he did it.

It was later that week that I received the life-changing phone call from the doctor. By this time, I was finishing my second year of university, living at home with my parents and older sister, who was engaged. My two brothers were already married and not living at home any more. I had a boyfriend of four years, a best friend, and a circle of good friends. And I was being told that a four-centimetre tumour had been found in the lower back portion of my stomach and that it was malignant. While my cancer was discovered in a late stage, the diagnosis was a miracle. I most definitely would not be here today to share my perspective on caregiving if it weren't for one dedicated ER doctor who believed there was more going on with me beyond the mere stress of being a young university student.

At the age of twenty-one, I was diagnosed with stomach cancer. I was scheduled for surgery two weeks later. It was hard for me to grasp what was happening. I went from being a vibrant young woman who enjoyed school, worked as a waitress, and loved all the things that young adults love doing — dancing all night at clubs, hanging out in coffee shops talking to girlfriends about postgraduate plans, living a life that I was not at all ready to be tossed — to a cancer patient, almost overnight.

While I had a large circle of support, there were many moments throughout my journey when I felt utterly alone. My hope is that in sharing my story, I can help others understand the emotional and mental state of a patient. Throughout the various stages, I felt alone, despite having so many people around me. Often, on the surface situations may appear stable, but underneath lies a different beast; a caregiver may not know exactly how their loved one is truly feeling.

When I was first diagnosed, I didn't fully grasp what had happened. Denial protects us for a bit, so it was as though I was living in some sort of altered state. I knew I had cancer because I was told I had it, but I did not yet feel like a patient, and physically I still looked and felt the same. I suppose the same was true for my caregivers; they knew that their loved one, daughter, sibling, friend had cancer, but the reality and the gravity of the situation took a while to fully sink in … for all of us.

BRING AN ADVOCATE

In the first few weeks leading up to the surgery, my family was always close by and accompanied me to many doctor's appointments and preop visits. This was valuable to me because as the patient I would tend to tune out what was being said. There was too much information being thrown at me all at once, so it was very important to have others at my appointments, not only for the emotional support but also for the mental support to ensure that of all the information was captured and understood and that the right questions were being asked and answered.

SHOW COMPASSION, NOT PITY

One of the most difficult aspects of being a cancer patient was dealing with the stigmas that are attached to cancer. As soon as anyone hears the "C-word," people act differently. Tones of voice change, facial expressions are sympathetic, people just react differently to you when they find out you have cancer. For this reason, especially in the beginning, the care recipient may not be ready to accept the fact that they are sick and need help. They may want to hang on to whatever independence they have until they absolutely can't. I was not ready to feel vulnerable and accept the help of others because in my mind I did not need the help yet. I still felt fine. As a caregiver, this can be a tricky road to navigate, but I do believe that you should try your best to insert yourself into the care recipient's appointments and be there for them without overdoing it and becoming a "helicopter caregiver" right off the bat. Your loved one will thank you for it afterward.

Also, understand that while they may say they are okay, they are internalizing out of necessity and need time to accept the changes that are happening. Try to remember that they are facing the fact that the future they had envisioned for themselves has at the least been put on hold and may never become a reality. As a newly diagnosed cancer patient, I was grieving the loss of the plans I had set out. The backpacking trip I was planning to go on the month after my diagnosis — plane tickets bought and hostels booked — all needed to be cancelled. I was grieving the loss of my third year of university. I was grieving the loss of possibly getting married and having children. My whole future was in question. Would I be alive to see any of it?

The day of my surgery felt like a sequel to the movie *My Big Fat Greek Wedding*, only we were mostly Portuguese and there was nothing to be celebrating that morning. It was just a big, messy family event. I rolled into the surgical check-in section with my entourage of close to twenty people. There were my parents, siblings, their partners, my boyfriend, my boyfriend's parents, and my friends. It really was quite the funny spectacle, if it wasn't so heartbreaking. I have to admit, as crazy as we must have looked to others, within this massive group of people I felt encircled in love, and I felt safe. I knew that in about ten hours, once I woke up, my life would be forever changed. It was comforting to know that at least the people around me, my loved ones, would still be there, and that was not changing.

The days after surgery were very painful and foggy, but my immediate family was there, and just their presence in the room brought a deep sense of comfort.

REMEMBER, GESTURES SMALL GO A LONG WAY

On the day after surgery, my sister came in to visit with some gifts. She had gone out and bought a couple of kerchiefs. Without even knowing what my staging was or if I would need to undergo chemo, she bought the kerchiefs and we wore them preemptively together all day. She said that no matter what I was going to have to go through, she would be there with me. This small gesture of solidarity spoke louder than words. While neither she nor anyone else understood what I was going through, she was showing me that she was there by my side and ready to lend the support I was going to need.

LEAN IN CLOSER WHEN IT GOES FROM BAD TO WORSE

A few days after my surgery, my surgeon came in to deliver the pathology results and the news of my staging. It was on that day that my life officially changed. I went from a young woman who just had seventy-five percent of her stomach removed but was still hopeful for her future to a young woman who had just had most of her stomach removed and was now being told that she might not even have a future. I was diagnosed with Stage 3b stomach cancer and was given a five-year survival rate of fifteen to twenty percent. I would need to undergo six months of chemotherapy and twenty-five consecutive days of radiation.

This news was beyond devastating for me and my caregivers. How were my loved ones supposed to act around me now? Were they supposed to stay optimistic and say that everything would be all right? Or were they supposed to cry and show me the fear that they were most definitely feeling? And how was I supposed to act? Everyone, at least on the surface, remained positive and never shared how they might have truly been feeling. Perhaps it was for this reason that I never shared with them how I was really feeling.

My first few weeks at home were physically very difficult. I had a lot of trouble just sitting up and walking. Having been cut right down the centre of my abdomen made a lot of everyday tasks very difficult. For a few weeks, I slept in my sister's bed with her. I told everyone it was because I might need help getting up in the middle of the night to go to the bathroom, but the truth was I was afraid of being alone because I was afraid of dying. I'm so grateful she leaned in and didn't pull away.

SLEEP RITUALS ARE CRITICAL

When I eventually graduated to my own bed, my fear of death did not dissipate, and I came up with another way to cope: I started meditating and envisioning my stomach as a Pac-Mac man game with little Pac-Men eating away at any rogue cancer cells in my body. I also began to read about miracles. I read every passage in the Bible that told a story of a miracle, and I read the book *Chicken Soup for the Surviving Soul*, which one of my friends had given to me when I was diagnosed. My secret nightly rituals were providing me with the strength and courage to fall asleep at night and wake up the next day feeling a bit more optimistic than the night before.

SHARE SECRETS AND BE HONEST

Looking back, I know that I kept my nightly routine a secret because I was afraid to share it with my caregivers, who to me seemed to all be handling my prognosis so well. How could I share how scared I was if no one around me seemed scared? I felt like I could not open up to anyone because no one else was really opening up to me. It's hard to say if I would have shared my secret even if my caregivers had been more open with me. Maybe I still would have kept it a secret, but after years of thinking about it, I would most definitely say that as a caregiver, you should try to be open and share how you are feeling, as tactfully as possible. It allows the patient to share their own fear.

Don't be negative, pessimistic, or show sheer panic, but don't be afraid to sit down and be as open and honest as you can. Please take this advice sensitively. Be mindful of your care recipient's emotional and physical state. Don't sit them down on a day that they are not in a good frame of mind or are physically having a bad time. Wait for a time when they are in a frame of mind to hear what you are feeling and what you are going to share. While the conversation may be tough on both of you, laying it all out there and letting the care recipient know how you are doing can open up a space for them to share what they are feeling and fearing. If, for whatever reason, your care recipient does not react well to you sharing how you feel, or if you see that it's leading them into a negative space, back off a bit; maybe it is not the right time. But at least try to create an opening for authentic conversation, because it is highly likely they need to talk too.

If just one of my caregivers had opened up a bit more and talked to me about what they were going through, I might have felt as though I could reciprocate and talk to them too. I was yearning for a circle of trust with someone, but I did not want to initiate the conversation. I believed that they couldn't handle it, and they were probably feeling like I couldn't. In retrospect, we all would have benefitted from this level of emotional vulnerability, and we could have helped each other better navigate the emotions that inevitably come with such a difficult journey.

As time went on and I moved toward the latter part of my treatments — around five months after my surgery — I began to fully feel the effects of being a gastric cancer patient. I had lost over forty pounds and was literally skin and bones. I felt sick, and I looked sick. At five feet eight inches and barely ninety pounds, I was definitely making heads turn. I looked frail and unwell for someone my age. I only left the house to go to the hospital for treatments. Any other outing was just not worth the physical effort or the emotional strain of worrying what people were thinking about my appearance. As time passed, I felt more and more sick, more and more like a person who was fighting for her life, and yet it seemed to me that everyone around me was going on with their lives as usual. As I was getting sicker, I felt like everyone was forgetting about me and what I was going through. It was hard for me to have visits from friends and hear about superficial things like their days at school, what projects they were working on, or what professor was upsetting them. It was hard for me to hear my parents walking around the house going about their day-to-day routines while I lay in bed, too weak to sit up and take a sip of water. In my sickest moments, I felt the most alone, secluded from the world around me. Sometimes it felt surreal as I was just watching everyone around me thrive, but I could not be a part of it. I'm not resentful that my caregivers went on living their lives, but I do want to shed light on how I felt as a patient and my perception at the time, as irrational as it may have been. The fact that I felt I couldn't talk to anyone about my deeper feelings left me feeling confused and isolated. So as much as I wanted things to remain as normal as possible and didn't want to be treated as a cancer patient, as time went on and as my condition worsened, I began to resent it when people acted as though it was business as usual, so to speak.

PAY CLOSE ATTENTION

Timing is everything, and as a caregiver you will want to be aware of the stage your loved one is in; there will be good weeks and bad weeks; things will progress and then worsen. Be aware of the hard times and be sensitive to the fact that while you still need to go to work and you still need to take care of the kids and all the other things you need to do in your life on top of being a caregiver, your care recipient may begrudge you the very fact that you still have your daily routines and activities. That is exactly why I feel that being a caregiver is probably one of the toughest jobs there is. You have to be mindful of how your care recipient may be feeling day to day, you have to keep your own life on track, and often you don't know whether acting "normally" or sharing your day with your loved one is the right thing to do. Here's the big secret: neither do we. It is a trial and error, day-by-day game.

BE THANKFUL FOR THE BORING AND NORMAL

One of the things that would upset me the most was when any of my friends or family would complain about being bored or about their day at work.

Complaints about life in general really did not sit well with me during my treatment months, because I would have given anything in the world to be bored or to have a bad day at work or to be dealing with the stress of school. I would have done anything to be living a normal life again, as opposed to fighting for my life and feeling horrible. I never vocalized my feelings to anyone because I was too worried about hurting other people's feelings or scaring them. Who was I to be upset for someone visiting me and taking the time to sit and tell me about their day? Instead, I just listened, because I knew that they were not intentionally trying to hurt or upset me. They were just trying to make conversation and be normal around me. Normalcy is often something that, as a patient, we wish so greatly to have back in our lives. A "normal" life, a life without hospitals and doctors and dependency on others to do everyday things.

SHOW YOUR EMOTIONS

I wish that my parents communicated with me differently while I was a patient and showed their emotions differently. Growing up, we never really showed any affection in the house; we never told each other we loved each other. I never hugged or kissed my parents — at least not as a teen or young adult. I know that my parents suffered as my caregivers; I could hear the crying, I could hear the conversations they had on the phone talking about my situation and how scared they were to lose their child at such a young age. I knew they were dealing with a lot, but we never really shared anything with each other, verbally or physically. Now, as a parent myself, I can empathize with what they must have been going through and how difficult it was for them. My parents cared for me in the best way they knew how; they ensured I was always comfortable and warm in the house, they would try to force to me to eat and drink (even though that was the last thing I wanted many days), they drove me to my appointments and waited patiently as I had treatments. And while they were never overly affectionate or ones to talk about their feelings, there were some special moments. It's these particular moments with a caregiver that say so much, and while I wish I had more of these to share, I will tell you about the one moment that did mean the world to me.

It happened on my first day of receiving dual treatment. My first two months of treatment were solely chemotherapy, but by my third month of chemo, my radiation treatment started. The doctors had warned me that the dual therapy would be tough on my body the first few days and that I should expect to feel very sick. That day, I had my radiation treatment first thing in the morning, and then had a two-hour wait for chemo. My parents and I sat together in the hospital atrium, making small talk until my chemo appointment. Later, I sat down in the chemo chair, the nurses started to hook me up to an IV, my mother sat down in front of me and my father next to me. Within a few minutes of the chemo being delivered into my body, I started to become very sick. Quickly, my mother grabbed a garbage pail, held it with one hand, and placed the other hand on my leg. My father moved behind me and held my hair so that it did not get covered in vomit. The two of them comforted me and told me that I would be okay. This one moment has stayed with me for years, and each time I think of it, I'm brought to tears because I can recall the love that I felt and the support that I had in that moment. It was a moment when actions spoke so much louder than words. It was not usual for my parents to be emotional and physical with me, but they let their guard down, and in that one moment I received what I had been longing for. A gesture beyond the comforts of your norm as a caregiver, a gesture that may appear to be small or insignificant to you, can most definitely mean so much more to your loved one.

KNOW THAT SOMETIMES TOUGH LOVE IS REQUIRED

Another example of a gesture that impacted me deeply was a moment of tough love. I was in the last week of my radiation treatments, and as the doctors had warned me, I was in a lot of pain. My esophagus and abdomen felt burned, and I could barely handle the pain of swallowing my own saliva. I had succumbed to lying in bed, and as hard as it is to admit it and say it out loud, I had come to terms with the very real possibility of dying. Having gone through the hard times and knowing what it felt like to be so utterly tired and in pain and not being able to see the light at the end of the tunnel, I understand how people may lose their strength to keep fighting. I only once ever reached the low of giving up, and let me tell you, it is a very dark place. What pulled me out of it was a moment of tough love from my sister; a moment that I don't think she even knew helped me so much. She had come home from work one evening, and I could hear her downstairs asking my parents if I had gotten out of bed that day. She came up the stairs, opened my door and said. "You smell, and you're giving up. Get up and get your ass in the bathtub!" She drew me a bath and forced me out of bed. I took that bath, and I literally washed my negativity away. I walked myself down the stairs with a renewed commitment to keep fighting. I was ready to keep moving forward.

EVOLVE WITH CAREGIVING

As a caregiver, you may be stretched beyond your limits, emotionally and physically, and the strain the role places on you may take its toll. But I would encourage you to let the new role and the journey you are on help you evolve as a person. Change happens best outside of your comfort zone, and while you may not have been looking to change, caregiving will change you whether you like it or not. You will be faced with new emotions and most likely forced into situations or discussions that are uncomfortable. Take these opportunities and set aside the potential negative aspects so you can turn them into positive experiences. I'm sure that my caregivers — my parents, my family, and my friends — all dealt with emotions they had never felt before and had to find a way to process them and deal with them. Perhaps they opened up to each other to deal with their feelings, but they did not include me, which left me feeling isolated, alone, and like an outsider.

SHOW YOUR VULNERABILITY

I started my story by saying that there are two things I believe all caregivers should do. The first is to be open and vulnerable with your loved one about your emotions and how you are handling the situation. Being open and transparent may provide your loved one with a safe place that will allow him or her to feel comfortable to share with you, even if it's just admitting to your care recipient that you don't know whether you should act normal, or that you don't know what to talk about now, that the typical day-to-day stuff seems so superficial and irrelevant. Perhaps your care recipient will say that they want to pretend nothing is wrong, or maybe they will use the opening to talk about what's really going on inside of them.

GO BEYOND THE SUPERFICIAL

The second thing I believe all caregivers should do is regularly ask your care recipient how they are doing. And when they give you an answer, ask again, "How are you *really* doing?" You might even want to say, "On a scale of 1 to 10, 1 being the worst you've ever been since the diagnosis and 10 being the best, what would your rating be today?" The idea is to get out of the superficial questions and answers and into a sit-down-and-get-serious, let's-get-real-and-peel-back-the-layers-of-the-onion kind of conversation. By doing this and showing that you really want to know and are truly willing to accept the answers you get, your loved one will get the opportunities they may be longing for to open up. I had a lot of love and support during my journey, and there were a lot of people in my circle, but I never had that one person who really asked me how I was doing, and because of that, I never felt like I could share how scared I was or how I was coping.

* * *

Transparency, openness, and heartfelt communication are what build the foundation for a strong partnership between caregiver and care recipient. At the end of it all, you will do and give as much as you can to your loved one. You can't really go wrong when you are giving and showing love. Being there for your loved one, doing all that you can do, will mean more than you can imagine. However, as with all things in life, we can always learn from others' experiences and pick up a nugget or two from someone else's advice. And I hope you will be able to do just that from my journey and my feelings.

Eighteen years after my cancer diagnosis, I am married to the most incredible man (who I met two years after my diagnosis) and am mom to an amazing little girl. It was quite a road to recovery, physically and emotionally. Postsurgery, I realized that I had to turn my life around in order to avoid relapse and in order to give myself the best possible chance to be part of the twenty percent who survived this diagnosis. I turned to fitness, nutrition, and good habits to make myself as strong as I possibly could so I would never have to go through this nightmare again. Fitness is something I turned to initially when I was fighting for my life, but now I can say fitness is what saved my life. I don't know how many times I was told how lucky I am. I was being given a second chance, and I had to do everything I could to take advantage of that. Fitness has played such an integral role in my recovery and growth as a person, and I owe my mental well-being and my physical strength to it. I am now a certified fitness instructor, and for a few hours a week I am gifted with the ability to provide my participants with a time that allows them to work on themselves, to forget their stresses in life, to get whatever it is that they need when they come to class. In my own little way, I feel like a caregiver every time I teach, because my participants trust me to fulfill their needs.

My husband, while he was not one of my caregivers when I was going through my recovery and treatments, was, and still is, one of my main supporters in life. For the three years after I met him, he accompanied me to my six-month scans and follow-up appointments. He was my shoulder to cry on and my rock to provide me with strength and support as I awaited the results of my scans every six months leading up to my five-year postdiagnosis mark. We did have the deep conversations; he shared with me how he felt, and he allowed me the comfort to share with him how I felt. There was no hiding of fears or emotions. I was able to share with him my fear of death, my fear of not making it to the five-year mark, and I know I was able to share with him my feelings because he shared with me his. He would ask me how I felt, and he really wanted to know. He listened. He asked more questions. He shared his thoughts, his feelings, and his fears with me. The transparency, openness, and heartfelt communication are what built the foundation of our relationship and what continues to keep our relationship strong after all these years.

CHAPTER TWO

GIVE SO THERE'S SOMETHING LEFT

AMANDA GAGNE

Amanda Gagne was a teacher who cared so deeply about her special needs students that she forgot to take care of herself, and she blamed herself the day life pushed her so hard that she cracked. Now she is the one needing care, and she shares a unique perspective from both sides of the caregiver and also as the care recipient.

As part of my Character Education class, whether in grade one or grade eight, I would always start the year off with *The Giving Tree* by Shel Silverstein. If you don't know the book, the story is beautiful and follows the relationship between the tree and the boy throughout the boy's life. The tree loves the boy so much that it gives all it has to make the boy happy, until nothing is left but a stump. In the end, the boy grows into an old man and realizes the stump is all he needs. The class discussion always leads to the same conclusion: the tree was the "hero" because he gave everything he had to help the boy. Some students would determine the boy was selfish for asking from the tree until there was nothing left. But the overall message, the one I wanted them to take away, is that it is so important to give and help others in any way we can. But I have since learned that we cannot give until there is nothing left of ourselves, or for ourselves. The lesson I would teach now would help my students as they grow and develop their own sense of giving while maintaining their personal well-being above all else.

* * *

As anyone in the education field knows, our role as teachers has changed significantly over the years. While we still deliver the curriculum and build on children's intellectual ability, our role has morphed into much more than that. We must now work with, and build upon, our students' mental and emotional needs. Many of our students must have their basic emotional needs met before they are ready to accept the challenges of academic growth. Although I cannot speak to Teacher's Education now, this was never part of any learning as a teacher candidate over twenty years ago when I was getting my degrees. And so we were thrown into the fire of managing a class without being fully prepared for the mental and emotional challenges we would face. I graduated top of my class. I was ready and excited, but I was nowhere near prepared for what came next.

Over the next eighteen years, I dedicated myself to caring for these children. *My* children. They occupied my mind constantly. Every night, every weekend, every holiday, I put everything I had into helping them, planning for them, caring for them, to the detriment of my own health and my own family. I saw only the needs and demands of my classroom, the suffering and abuse of the children I was supposed to protect, and the intense need for them to experience a safe, loving environment. I saw the cut marks on a little boy's arm hidden beneath the long sleeves he wore. I wiped away the tears of a child in fear that when she got home, she would be beaten because her four-year-old sister made her miss the bus. I sat on the floor throughout lunch to hold the child that was seizing. Or the hand of the child I had chased as he ran out of the school into the roadway. I embraced the child who destroyed my classroom in a fit of rage and spoke quietly and gently to her until her breathing slowed, her shaking stopped, and her rage dissipated into tears. I could tell you so many more stories like this. I have had to work with Children's Aid Society and the police in efforts to protect these innocent children more times than I should ever have had to. I am a classroom teacher, trained to educate and evaluate these children through effective delivery of the curriculum. But in today's classroom, I was responsible for so much more.

Jay was one such child. He was only five, yet his mental, emotional, and cognitive development was not that of a five-year-old. Although there was no diagnosis for a boy as young as he was, the developmental delays were evident. He was physically ready to be in my grade one classroom, but emotionally he was not at all as ready to adapt to the structures and routines as his peers were. Needless to say, academic learning was very low on his priority list. Every morning was a struggle to get him in the door without incident. His emotions were extreme, and he was incapable of self-regulation. He was not the only child in my class that year with serious emotional and behavioural difficulties, but he presented the most demands on my time and attention. Emotional outbursts occurred multiple times a day. He was a high flight risk — running out of the school and into the street was not an uncommon occurrence. It left me in a position of needing to make the difficult decision of which option presented the least danger — leaving him to run out into the street, not knowing where he was going, or giving a quick nod to the teacher next door as I left the other twenty-three children in my care to chase after one. It was a split-second decision, and either one could have serious consequences. Inevitably, I would always go after him because he was in the most imminent danger. There was no time to wait for help when he bolted out into the street.

Over the next few months, I would take his hand as he was running away, gently leading him back into the school. I would crawl under bathroom stalls, where he had climbed precariously to the top of the dividing walls, so I could lift him down to safety. I would sit in the hallway with him on the floor, holding his hand and talking gently after a fit of rage where he'd turned the classroom upside down. The torn-up papers, the broken pencils, the outbursts of rage and frustration; they all broke my heart because I could see through his outward manifestations of fear. I did everything I knew how. I set up a quiet room for him to access whenever he wanted. I helped him begin to recognize when his emotions were escalating and worked on strategies to help him cope. I gave him power by asking him to be part of determining the strategies we were going to try. I was slowly but surely gaining his trust. He began to smile. He began to engage in learning tasks to the best of his ability. He began to hug me in the mornings. He began to find his confidence. I use the word "began" because it was a very slow progress and things were far from perfect, but going from multiple severe outbursts each day to just a few each week was definitely a step in the right direction. I felt good about the progress we were making. Until *that* day.

It was a Monday. It had evidently not been a good weekend for Jay as he entered the school in a rage. Even after I managed to help him calm down, I could tell through his body language and his facial expressions that this would be a day of struggle. There were several incidents that morning: throwing boots down the hallway, chasing another student with my metre stick, crumpled papers, broken pencils, etc. Such mornings played on my self-esteem. I was feeling defeated, not necessarily by that morning's events, but by the overall build-up of exhaustion, self-criticism, and feeling over-whelmed. At recess, I took a moment alone to breathe deeply, but I was not prepared for what was waiting for me as I returned to the classroom.

I could hear him before I could see him. Jay was screaming in the hallway as another teacher was firmly leading him to me. I never really got the whole story as she was speaking in a loud, firm voice and he was screaming above it all. With all the other children in the hallway getting undressed, it was chaos. I tried to calm him down, but his outburst was beyond what I could handle, so I buzzed the office for help. The principal came immediately, but all we could do was protect the other students as we watched and waited while he ripped posters from the wall, tipped desks, threw chairs, and continued his outburst until he was exhausted. It was almost ten minutes until I could approach him safely. When I finally did, I took his hand and we walked to the office. I led him to the sick room, where we sat on the bench. He was still shaking and out of breath, but his immense anger was subsiding. The principal told him she was going to have to call home. He screamed, "NO!" and began getting agitated again. I explained that there was no choice this time. He started crying and scrambled under the bench we were sitting on. When the father flew through the door and past the principal's office, completely ignoring her, I understood his immense terror. The father was screaming obscenities and calling Jay names no child should ever have to hear. He had a stroller with three younger children in it, witnessing it all and not even flinching. I guess that tells its own story. He grabbed Jay's arm and yanked him out from under the bench, not even caring that he smashed his little head against the metal legs in the process. We tried to stop him.

After they left, I was in shock. I acted on autopilot as I wrote my report. After calling the Children's Aid Society, I returned to the classroom, but the second I walked through the doorway, I dropped. I just didn't have it in me any more. I completely broke. The principal sent me home and to the doctor that day. She had sensed my progressive breakdown, but I wouldn't listen. I would *not* be that teacher who failed. Who couldn't do it. Except I was. And I have not been back to the classroom since.

GOING FROM CAREGIVER TO ONE IN NEED OF CARE

November 30, 2015 was the day I began a whole new journey of self-discovery.

It has not been an easy journey; far from it. The road has been long and filled with the slow, arduous steps up the mountains and the slippery, uncontrollable slides back down into the valleys. It has taken a lot of work, support, and introspection to get to where I am now. Although I occasionally catch glimpses of the peak, I know there is still a long way to climb, but it is not in vain because I now know what it means to be on both sides. As a caregiver, I can now see where I went wrong and what I need to do not only to care for others, but also to care for myself.

Over the past three years, I have been diagnosed with several mental illnesses, and as a result, I have had many caregivers. I have had doctors, a psychologist, social workers, psychiatrists, therapists, psychotherapists, nurses, and even family and friends. I have had good experiences, and I have had bad ones. I am grateful for all of my caregivers, the ones I have connected with and the ones I haven't, because they have all helped me to learn what it means to be a truly inspiring, effective, and impactful caregiver.

WHAT A CARE RECIPIENT NEEDS

The qualities I have found in effective caregivers are ones that relate to a way of "being," as opposed to "knowing." Although I do believe education and training are a very important foundation, the best caregivers I have had are the ones who understand beyond what can ever be gained through coursework. They are the ones who relate on a deeper, human level.

Some of the things that have been very helpful, and very important to me as the care-recipient are as follows:

LISTEN TO HEAR

It is important as a caregiver to listen for the sake of hearing and not just for the sake of responding. I have had therapists who are not deeply listening. Ones who cut me off midsentence, who continually interrupt. It is disheartening. It makes me feel unheard. Invalidated. In moments when I am opening up and being vulnerable, I want to feel accepted. It doesn't mean they always agree. In fact, they often don't. But to be an effective caregiver, before offering a point of view, it is important to truly try to understand. When I feel heard and understood, when I feel validated and worthy, only then can I start seeing the situation from other perspectives.

CHALLENGE ME

Many times, my caregivers have listened, validated, but have been able to challenge my perspective, or my "truth." They have turned situations around, made analogies relating to my own experiences, and helped me to see different angles. The very best caregivers, the ones I have learned the most from, take me to the edge. They challenge my thoughts and beliefs in a firm manner and yet have the compassion and respect to understand when I express my inability to go any further.

SHOW VULNERABILITY

As a caregiver, be vulnerable. Show me your human side. Tell me a personal story about a time you faced adversity and how you triumphed. Show me it is possible. This gives me hope because you are real to me. I am listening, I am watching, and I am learning. I need hope that my situation can improve. That I can overcome some of my challenges. That I can still have a good life. Show me you have had times of struggle too, because by sharing your own difficulties, you are allowing me to see I am not alone. As a professional, I realize self-disclosure must be used with caution and that you are not able to share current personal struggles with a client. But sharing stories of how you worked to resolve difficult situations, or how you are still challenged by aspects of your own life, helps me to accept my own imperfections.

HOLD YOUR BOUNDARIES

Please hold your boundaries. In doing this, you are a role model for me to develop and maintain my own boundaries. This was one of the biggest contributing factors to my breakdown. I could not develop and maintain personal boundaries to protect myself against all of the hurt and heartbreak from not being able to protect all of the students in my class. I have since learned that giving more than you have to others leaves you with nothing left to give to yourself and to your own family.

CARE FOR YOURSELF

Above all else, care for yourself. My very best caregivers have enough care and compassion to extend to me because they care for themselves first. They take time to rest, rejuvenate, and engage in activities that make them happy. I never understood until now what people meant by "you can't truly love others until you love yourself first," but I do understand now. If you don't take care of yourself first and foremost, there will come a time when you have nothing left to extend to others. Pouring from an empty cup is impossible, and like the Giving Tree, when there is nothing left of you, there is nothing to give to others who are in need of your help.

* * *

I won't lie. It's not always easy accepting this reversal of roles, going from caregiver to one in need of care. I long for the day I can make it back to the other side of the line. But then I wonder, is there really a line? Does there have to be? I mean, shouldn't we all embrace both roles and find the blessings in each? To be able to care for people around us is a very acceptable, respected role in society. But aren't we all in need of care sometimes? Don't we all need someone to help us through the difficult chapters of our lives? Why do we not embrace this role as much as we do the other? Why do we feel failure when we need to rely on someone else? The human connection is one of give and take. We cannot go through life giving everything we have, just as we can't go through life taking everything from everyone else. There is no shame in needing help. For me, being deeply rooted in both sides of this line has been a blessing. I can understand the needs, the struggles, and the soul-filling experiences from both sides. What I have learned is that I am human. Perfectly imperfect, just like everyone else.

CHAPTER THREE

CAREGIVING TAKES CARE RECEIVING

PENNY TREMBLAY

As speaker, author, and entrepreneurial mom, Penny Tremblay talks about the challenges involved in receiving help from a live-in caregiver to care for her children. She imparts several powerful lessons as she very honestly shares the deep internal fears and struggles of sharing her caregiver role with another woman. These lessons include the importance of receiving.

G iving, giving, giving. That's what caregivers do, but giving and receiving are like both sides of your hand — you can't have one without the other, and as it turns out, receiving isn't as easy as one would think. As it turns out, most caregivers could learn to be better receivers, including me. But eventually, I realized that the circle of abundance is not complete only with giving. We must also be open, willing, and able to receive. The energy needs to be flowing in and out, continuously through an open channel. Since the launch of my book, *Give and Be Rich*, most of my conversations with people and audiences are based on the challenges we have when it comes to receiving the abundance that life has to offer. To illustrate, I will share my personal caregiving experience of learning how to receive, and give, in important ways that I hadn't really considered up until then.

Caregiving and care receiving are like a dance, where at times one person leads and then allows themselves to be led; all must be open, trusting, vulnerable, and willing to go with the flow, accepting what comes in, as well as what goes out. And to also accept that stepping on each other's toes once in a while is all part of learning to dance.

* * *

"Congratulations, Penny! You're pregnant."

Finally! The time in my life had come where I was going to be a mom. I was going to be a giver of care; I was going to be that infinite supply of everything my little bundle needed. I was elated and terrified all at the same time. My, oh my, how my life was going to change. I owned and operated a full-time business, and my husband was also a business owner. I didn't know how we would manage it all, but after freaking out for a little while, we got to talking to somebody who had a live-in caregiver from the Philippines who lived with their family and helped take care of the children as well as the home. I had always thought live-in caretakers were for the wealthy (which we were not), but after some research, it seemed that it was not only a possibility but also perhaps the perfect solution for an entrepreneurial family like ours. We would get the extra needed support with childcare as well as with the household and still be able to meet the demands of our businesses, which included working evening and weekend hours when daycares were not available to provide care. A live-in caretaker sounded like the perfect solution to allow us more quality family time and a better work-life balance.

It took me almost a year to navigate the paperwork and regulations to arrange for and find a suitable candidate, but it was time well spent. Permission was granted, and Hazel was hired.

I'll never forget the day she arrived. She walked through our front door, exhausted from the flight. She was very shy and timid, but she had a big, radiant smile. She was nervous yet excited to meet us in person and begin the next chapter of her life. How brave of her to trust us as employers, to venture across the world, to leave her known way of life and family behind. I admired her courage.

I also was exhausted, nervous, and shy, yet excited to meet our new caregiver. How was this all going to work? Would we be able to communicate well? Was I going to be able to trust someone else with my baby? So many questions, so much excitement, yet so much trepidation and concern about taking the most precious gift that I have ever been given, my son, and allowing someone else to care for him while I worked.

We showed Hazel to her bedroom, and the next morning she was ready to begin her new role. To train her, I simply performed my new mom role as she observed and assisted alongside me for an entire week. She was gracious and kind, patient, and eager. She quickly took to our son and showed great interest in him, his happiness, and his care. And he quickly took to her.

Within a few short weeks, Hazel had mastered *everything* involved in becoming our family's caregiver. She took care of my son and helped me tremendously. It was like having another me to take care of the family and the house, and just like me, she even fell in love with our dog.

As pleased as I was that she quickly mastered *my* new mom role, I was also insecure. I didn't share this secret with anyone — not even the dog! I just tried letting the gratitude of having such great help take precedence over my feelings of inadequacy at perhaps not being as good a caregiver to my child as she was. She was such a natural at it. I was a rookie. I sometimes thought she had a magic wand that she waved over the house, making everything fall into its place. She performed her caregiver role with such ease and grace — much more so than I did.

DON'T HOLD IT INSIDE

I deeply loved my new family, and I wanted to make a beautiful home for them and to conform to our mutual decision to hire a live-in caregiver. But it wasn't always easy to make room for another woman who was much better at performing *my* role and responsibilities than I was. It was incredibly intimidating at times and poked at my doubts of being enough.

Within a few short months of Hazel's arrival, I was blessed with another pregnancy and soon thereafter welcomed our beautiful daughter. The need for Hazel's care grew exponentially. We tag-teamed the responsibilities of an infant and a toddler: two diaper bags, two cribs, two high chairs, and two different meals for each of them as they went through those early years. When I wasn't there, I could always rely on Hazel, and it felt satisfying to know that Hazel could also rely on me. We invested a lot of time, energy, and communication into our relationship. I could tell she felt comfortable asking me for anything that would help her with her job, help her feel welcome and comfortable, help her to be mobile on her days off, and to meet new friends and establish her new life here in Canada.

As time went on, Hazel grew strong roots as our family caregiver, earning the love of my children. A big part of me was happy to have provided and established a stable environment for my kids while managing my business and allowing my spouse to manage his, but another part of me was still worried that the kids might love Hazel more than me, or that she'd earn more respect than I would for being the solid provider of care when I was away for business. To top off the insecurities, the lack of self-worth and guilt tainted the gratitude of having both a family and business. The balance wheel was wobbly, and it wasn't just my own thinking either. There was pressure that I felt from my husband, in-laws, some friends, and even strangers on occasion, which served to intensify my feelings of being torn between my work life and family life. Although we're all told we shouldn't care what other people think, and we should ignore their judgements of us, it is one of those things that's easier said than done. I suppose in hindsight, I was also judging myself.

Regardless of anyone's judgements, including my own, I knew I wanted more than anything to be The One for my kids, but I also knew that I needed the personal satisfaction and sense of purpose that came from working outside of the home. I wasn't the best one to stay home, so allowing someone else to be the caregiver for my precious family was a silent battle that regularly played out in my mind.

ACKNOWLEDGE EMOTIONS

It took a long time for me to realize that I had to receive Hazel's care in a deeper sense. To fully "receive" her care, I had to acknowledge my own feelings of inadequacy, and I had to stand in the idea of being worthy and deserving of such great care for our family *and* having an amazing career. I had to allow everything that came from this situation to land, including all of the unpleasant emotions, and to really unpack it all. I had to resolve this inner conflict that had been brewing silently for so long.

Some parents choose to stay home and raise their children, while others choose to take their young ones to daycare, and some, like me, choose to hire a live-in caregiver. In any of the options, there's potential for inner conflict because we need to surrender to the fact that we need help, not necessarily want help, but *need* it. Receiving help and the challenges that come with it were humbling. I had to dig deeper than I ever had before and learn to really stand in the decisions that I had made for my kids, my family, and myself. I didn't realize it at the time, but even feeling worthy and deserving of having someone provide me with top-notch care was daunting. It was a balancing act in humility, not being above or beneath the opportunity to have someone care for me and my family.

I was eventually able to accept the fact my insecurities had nothing to do with Hazel and everything to do with my past conditioning and the meaning I'd attached to being a good mother. I realized the negative things I had made it mean about me wanting to continue to be an entrepreneur and also wanting to take care of my own needs while having a family.

RECEIVE WHOLEHEARTEDLY

It was very apparent that Hazel had a desire to be a caregiver and wasn't taking on the role just for a paycheque or for an opportunity to immigrate to Canada. She truly loved her Canadian family, and it showed. You could taste it in the food she cooked. You could see it in the way that she attended to the children and cared for the home. The love she put into everything made it easier to fully accept and receive her care.

Life has many currencies, and when I made the conscious decision to open myself fully to the giving and receiving of my caregiving situation, I gained an incredible amount of value from Hazel. Most lucrative for me was learning the value of receiving wholeheartedly without fear, insecurity, resentment, or other negative emotions. I remember saying that I wanted to be just like her when I grew up, and the funny thing about that is I am older than her. Hazel was a hardworking, honest, spiritual, giving person who also knew how to receive graciously. She came from an extended family culture. A culture where many family members lived under the same roof. Parents, grandparents, children, married spouses, nieces, nephews, and grandchildren all living within same residence, where everyone had to give and receive in order to thrive in the situation. This was very different from anything I'd experienced growing up. In my childhood we had Mom and Dad in our house, and our grandparents didn't live too far away. We had aunts and uncles and cousins nearby and often gathered for large family events, but we didn't live together. I often wondered how people in extended family cultures had the patience and tolerance to get along under one roof, and I realized through observing Hazel that people learn patience and tolerance, as well as the art of giving and receiving, when living in a community with others. There seemed to be a beautiful culture growing out of extended families, where sharing and caring opportunities went hand in hand. Hazel continued to contribute both to our family and to her own back home, regularly sending money to assist her family members. This is one of the benefits of an extended family culture: people all contribute to support one another. When Hazel needed funds to travel to her new job in Canada, her family supported her. With her earnings in Canada, she gave back.

What I learned from watching Hazel's way of being, mannerisms, and behaviour taught me so much. I admired how respectful she was. I watched how quietly she could manoeuvre in and amongst the family, and how almost invisible she could be when she didn't want to mingle. I learned also how important it was for her to have her alone time, her time away, and her time off. I also learned about simplicity. When she arrived, all her possessions fit into a suitcase, and then they grew to decorate a small bedroom, yet she was so very happy. I remember asking her one day, "Hazel, what would you like for Christmas?" Her answer? Peace. Hazel simply wanted peace. Again, I just yearned to be more like Hazel when I grew up. When we would go on weekend adventures, Hazel's stuff would fit into one backpack. She had very few possessions yet never felt like she was bereft. She was a giver of herself, and I grew so much from her example. She was a hard worker, very involved in her faith, and enjoyed time with community.

Looking back to when she first arrived, I was worried about how I'd cope with having her help, but that eventually changed to worrying about how I would cope *without* her help.

Ultimately, learning to be a better care receiver made me a better care-giver. I've learned that when I am fully open to receiving care, I grow rich in ways that are better than anything I could have imagined.

EMBRACE THE CIRCLE OF ABUNDANCE

I wonder if caregivers are willing to receive as much as they give? And I wonder if those receiving their care understand how much they are giving back in the circle of abundance.

I wonder if caregivers feel worthy and deserving of being cared for, or of taking the time to care for themselves, or of receiving far beyond money and material things? People who constantly give and become conditioned to offering the outflow of their energy and don't always understand the importance of the other side of the circle of abundance, which is receiving the inflow of energy. They often find themselves burned out, unsatisfied, and unfulfilled, insecure and confused because they're giving all they have. However, receiving is a process of allowing, and often, when who we are is all about other people, our own needs of physical, mental, emotional, and spiritual wellness suffer, and we eventually end up bankrupt.

As the receiver of Hazel's care, along with my children, I recognize that I also had to give in recognizable ways. I had to give my trust and my service back to Hazel to tend to her social needs and provide a place for her friends to gather so she could enjoy her time off and begin a new life here in Canada. The less noticeable giving I had to do was in the vulnerability that I had to display with sharing the role of mom with the possibility that my kids would love her more than me and share the acknowledgement of my spouse for a home well cared for. I had to give into my fears and insecurities of not being good enough and allow the insecurities that I had to surface in my mind and my heart.

Life's greatest gifts don't always come wrapped in attractive paper and aren't delivered with a smile and words of gratitude. Some of life's most impactful gifts are lessons learned from challenging experiences that help us blossom into the best versions of ourselves. These types of gifts are often riddled with frustration, fear, and feelings of being frozen in the discomfort that growth pushes us through. But if we can receive them openly and graciously, we are more in alignment with our heart and soul and less engaged with our ego.

Receiving is our own responsibility, and when we fully open ourselves to all of the experiences being offered and seek the blessings and the lessons that we can gain, we become rich in ways that we would never have thought possible.

When Hazel gave our family such great care, I had to allow myself to receive it, and although awkward at first, over time it filled me up enough to want to give back and take care of her as a member of our family. We needed each other. We needed to learn to give and receive caregiving in a healthy way. Giving and receiving are actually one and the same when you really get down to recognizing the dynamic flow of energy, in and out, back and forth, up and down; the circle of abundance has many directions and need not be stuck in only one.

* * *

There are two sides to healthy caregiving, one that gives and one that receives, and as long as we keep the channels of both fully open and allow the energy to flow freely and abundantly through our hands, our minds, our hearts and our souls, we will be abundant in all that really matters. Caregiving is an art, not a science. It will never be perfect, nor does it have to be, but we do grow rich in caring for one another.

CHAPTER FOUR

THE CONSCIOUS CAREGIVER

LISE LEBLANC

Not all of us know how or why we became caregivers, but in this profound personal account, Lise Leblanc, author of The Conscious Caregiving Guide, shares how her emotional baggage subconsciously affected her "decision" to become a caregiver. With heightened self-awareness, she realized how her traumatic past experiences were driving her motivations to care for others. But by doing her own internal work, Lise became a more conscious human being and a much more conscious caregiver. And you can too.

Some people can tell you the exact moment they decided to become a caregiver and the precise reasons why. Others cannot. I fell into the latter category, and for many years, I truly thought I'd landed in this career by sheer coincidence.

I was twenty-one years old when a friend who was a registered practical nurse asked if I would be interested in providing personal care to a young woman who was severely affected by cerebral palsy. The job involved total care and included feeding tubes, diaper changes, and so much more. At first, I thought, *No way!* I told her I'd never done anything like that before. I asked, "Don't you need someone who is qualified for this type of work?" She said it was a special contract directly through the family, and they could choose whoever they wanted, regardless of qualifications. She went on to explain that they were more interested in finding a caring and compassionate person than someone with the proper credentials. I wasn't sure I'd be able to do the job, or that I even wanted to, and as much as I hate to admit it, money played a huge factor in my decision. The job paid fifteen dollars an hour, which was a lot of money back then, and as an unemployed and almost starving student, I figured it was at least worth a shot.

In all honesty, I barely survived the first day of training. My friend decided it would be best to teach me the more challenging aspects of the job first to see if I could handle it. So it was a suppository and diaper change right off the hop. I'd never even changed a baby's bottom before! The tears welled up in my eyes as I fought off the urge to gag. I almost walked out but somehow pushed through. I'm not sure what brought me back (or kept me there for almost three years) other than the fact that I really clicked with this young lady and her family. But I'm glad I did, because I am left with so many fond memories of my time with her and also grateful for the fact that this decision launched me into a whole different career path — oddly, from law enforcement to caregiving. I'd already gone to college for policing, but once I completed my bachelor's degree in psychology and law, I became a therapist instead of a cop.

Professionally, I've worked as a therapist for the past twenty-two years. In my personal life, my caregiving roles included parenting my two children, now aged sixteen and twenty, and caring for my grandmother who had Alzheimer's disease for six years.

My whole adult life, I've been a caregiver, and for years I thought this all happened by chance. I had no idea how my past experiences were subconsciously driving my educational and career choices.

BY CHANCE OR BY PURPOSE

I grew up in a chaotic home environment where I felt I had no control. And I rebelled. I was a "behaviour problem." By fourteen, I was on probation for theft and breaking all the rules. I left home at fifteen because I couldn't stand authority, so it might seem ironic that I joined the military reserves at seventeen and went into the law and security program at Cambrian College. However, I have since realized that my choices were not as random as I'd thought. I was subconsciously choosing this career path as a way to gain authority. To eventually be the one in charge. To be in control. And I've also come to understand that my caregiving choices were not made by coincidence either. Let me explain...

At nineteen, I had completed my two-year college program and was nearing the end of my first year at Carleton University in Ottawa. Miraculously, I was doing well in school despite every other area of my life being a mess. I was at the end of a destructive relationship, and after two years together, I was drinking and smoking pot every day, I was sick with an eating disorder and suffering from anxiety and depression. I was suffering so much that I was seriously considering suicide because I didn't know what else to do. I had no hope that the future would get better, and I couldn't see any other options. Then, one night, in a moment of intense suffering, something strange happened. There I was, lying on my bed, thinking about all the things that were going wrong in my life, when for a brief instant I dissociated from myself. It was like an out-of-body experience. Suddenly, I was an impartial observer of a vaguely familiar character and her problematic life. Of course it was my life, but in this objective state, the problems I was having felt distant and unimportant. I felt so free without the heavy burden of all of the disempowering "stories" that were keeping me stuck.

During this eye-opening moment, I felt like there were two of me — the real me and my "story." I could see that the real me was covered by several layers of negative beliefs that I had about myself, about others, and about the world, all of which had been passed down to me when I was just a little girl. This was the very first time I'd ever considered the possibility that maybe, just maybe, I wasn't the bad, broken person I thought I was. I also wondered what my life would be like if I stopped believing all of this stuff. This is also when I realized that perhaps I was studying psychology to figure myself out!

Now, I'd love to tell you that once I had this ah-ha moment, I instantaneously pulled myself together and lived happily ever after, but that's not how it played out. I did start cleaning up my act — I broke up with the guy, moved back home, made amends with my parents, went to therapy for my eating disorder — but despite this new insight, I still had no idea how to find the sense of inner peace I'd experienced. So what I did was I tried to block out the trauma from my past and went on a mission to help others. Now I don't know if this makes sense to you, but at the time it somehow made sense to me to be out trying to heal others when I hadn't done my own internal work. Unfortunately, I know for a fact that I was not the only caregiver out trying to save others when I hadn't yet saved myself. I have come to learn that many caregivers are using their clients' problems as a distraction from their own, and many, including myself, subconsciously choose caregiving, either personally or professionally, as a way to avoid doing their own internal work.

HEAL PAIN FROM THE PAST

By the time I was thirty, I had everything. I was married, with two beautiful, healthy children. I had completed a master's degree. I was successful in my career as a therapist and manager. I was making great money. I was travelling, and my life was filled with luxuries. From the outside, I appeared happy and successful, but on the inside, I wasn't doing very well at all. I was burning out because the energy it took to repress my emotional wounds was depleting me and running on the hamster wheel was exhausting. So my response was to eat spinach, do yoga, go to the gym more often, take medication, and find more distractions (helping others). My understanding of self-care at the time was simply to take more time to pamper myself and do "healthy" things, but it turned out these were just more things to do, more appointments, more obligations, and more reasons to feel bad about myself when, for example,

I skipped a workout. I have nothing against these methods of self-care and do believe we should all take time to do nice things for ourselves: a bath, listening to music, finding a healthy distraction. These are all great strategies that will probably make you feel better for a while, but these things alone are not going to clear out the negative past experiences that are keeping you stuck and shutting you down. In my case, despite my "self-care" strategies, things continued to get progressively worse until I had a full-blown burnout. This is when my suffering pushed me into doing my own deep internal work to heal the pain from my past.

Now, your story may be very different than mine. Perhaps you had an amazing childhood or a great family life. But no matter how good your life has been up until now, no one gets through life completely unscathed. No matter how good you look on the outside, there's stuff going on the inside. And as my mentor always says, *If you're in the job of service, you need to make sure you're doing your own work.*

HEAL THE CHILD WITHIN

Inside of every person, there is a little boy or a little girl, and no matter how old you get, this inner child needs to be healed from the painful experiences and "stories" from the past. Otherwise, you will be perceiving and interpreting the world — and subconsciously choosing your relationships, career, and other pursuits — through the eyes of the unhealed child within.

I had no idea back then that this is what I was doing. I had no idea I had chosen psychology as a way to figure out my own issues or that I was focusing on my clients' problems as a way to hide from my own. But I have since learned that when you're hiding, you're not healing. I've also realized that in order to be an effective and conscious caregiver, you must dig deep down to the root of our own problems and clear out the old hurts, resentments, guilt and shame from the past. When we can get ourselves to the other side of our own pain, we are then in a position to pull our clients and care recipients through theirs.

CARE FOR THE CAREGIVER

It is a given that someone who is mentally, emotionally, physically, and spiritually taking care of themselves will be a much better caregiver. Therefore, here are three key ways to deal with your own issues so you can be a more effective and conscious caregiver:

1. DIG DEEP DOWN

The subconscious mind is a much more powerful processor than the conscious mind. It processes millions of bits of information. Its job is to filter and decide what is important for the conscious mind to be aware of on a massive scale every single second. The rest you don't have access to. And luckily so, because if you did, you would be overwhelmed and confused by this mass of largely irrelevant information — every morsel of food you ate; the cars, trees, and road signs you passed on your way to work; the faces and products you encountered at the grocery store; the colour of the car you parked beside at the mall, the name of your waiter at the restaurant, or how many times you used the restroom on any given day. You wouldn't be able to function if you couldn't filter and block out most of what comes in through your senses. The subconscious only brings to awareness the information your memories of past experiences and conditioning have programmed to consider important.

Until the age of seven, there is no filter between the conscious and the subconscious mind. As young children, we're given a bunch of information and we take it all in — you're good, you're bad, you're pretty, you're ugly, you're fat, skinny, smart, stupid — it all goes straight in. After the age of seven, the filter between the conscious and subconscious mind starts to develop, and the information coming in from the outside world gets filtered so not everything gets in. For example, if I told you the told story of Santa Claus for the first time today, you would not believe for a second that there's a fat guy in a red suit going around the world on a sled run by flying reindeers bringing gifts to billions of children in one night. But when you're five, you're like, *Wow, and he's gonna bring me presents if I'm good?* My point here is that Santa Claus is not the only lie that got into your subconscious mind. Based on what people told you and the meaning you attached to certain experiences in early childhood, these faulty beliefs still determine much of how you perceive and interpret "reality" in adulthood, and they continue to drive your thoughts, emotions, actions, and decisions. So whatever thoughts are haunting you about who you are, what you've done, what's happened to you, need to be pulled up and out of your subconscious mind.

Understand that for everything stopping you from going forward, there's something behind pulling you back. It's like having a rope attached to your waist, and every time you build up momentum, these past challenges and/or past conditioning pull you back. Unfortunately, most people create a world based on the script that was given to them and they find people who will help keep them in their act and help them play out the same movie over and over again, much like *Groundhog Day*. When you start to uncover and unravel the stories that are running rampant in your mind and start peeling back the layers of how your thinking is creating the same situations over and over again, you will start to recognize that you are the main character in your life, and you are the only one that can change the script you've been living to.

Until you get your unconscious mind working for you instead of against you, you'll feel like you're swimming upstream which takes a lot of energy. In your role as a caregiver, this will leave you feeling exhausted and at a loss as to how to truly make a difference in other people's lives.

2. REPROGRAM YOUR MIND

When we start paying attention to our thinking patterns, we notice how repetitive they are. It is very possible you are running the same negative, unproductive, fear-based thoughts over and over in your mind like a broken record. The cycle works like this: fearful thought pops up in your mind, anxious feelings arise which lead to more fearful thoughts, fear builds and more associated thoughts take root like weeds in a garden. This cycle continues until your whole nervous system is engaged and you are in full-blown fight-or-flight mode. Instead of redirecting our thoughts, most of us allow our minds to launch into anxieties about the future, regrets about the past, insecurities, assumptions, and judgements against ourselves and others. Since our thoughts affect how we feel, negative thinking patterns can easily lead us deep into the rabbit hole of self-doubt, anxiety, depression, and exhaustion, as well as a whole host of other problems. So how do we change our negative thinking, or at least slow it down?

We become so used to listening to the voice in our heads and believing everything it says that we often don't even notice it slowly poisoning us. We just jump on whatever thought train is going by without even thinking about where it's taking us. Before we can learn to consciously choose our thoughts, we must first notice them. So start listening to the voice in your head, because how you think will dictate how you feel. You can flood yourself with positive thoughts or negative thoughts, but remember, your emotions will follow your thoughts. So, take five minutes at least twice a day to do a simple mindfulness exercise. All you need to do is practice watching your thoughts without getting involved in them. When a thought arises, don't get onboard. Instead, just notice your thought and allow it to pass through your consciousness. Then spend five minutes with your care recipient in a total state of mindfulness, where you simply pay attention with presence to what is going on in the moment, without judgement.

3. CHANGE YOUR PATTERNS

When we habitually think, feel, and behave in certain ways, we become locked into a pattern and it becomes our default, meaning we are not consciously choosing our response but rather reacting by default. In other words, it's our "auto-pilot" mode. Changing a pattern is not easy. To demonstrate how difficult it is, take a moment to sign your name on a piece of paper. Once you've completed this task, rate its level of difficulty on a scale of one to ten (ten being most difficult). Go ahead and do it before reading any further. Now, sign your name with your other hand and again rate the level of difficulty. Unless you are ambidextrous, your rating will be much higher for your nondominant hand. That's because you've been signing your name with your dominant hand since you were about ten years old. Imagine how many times you would have to sign your name with your nondominant hand before it became as natural and comfortable as signing your name with your dominant hand. Recognizing how ingrained your default patterns have become and how difficult they are to change can help you realize why you don't always do better despite knowing better. For this reason, most will not stick with something new long enough for it to create a new pattern. But remember this … if nothing changes, nothing changes. In other words, if you're having the same conversations with the same people, doing the same things, thinking the same thoughts, you'll always get the same results.

If your current patterns are serving you well, then perfect, don't change anything. But if not, then consider making changes. Even if it's only small changes — take a different route to work, wear clothes you wouldn't normally wear, eat foods you don't like, talk to people you never do. Just consider the possibility that you are not who you think you are and that you're not locked into the role, the act, or the script you've been playing out.

* * *

As conscious awareness grows, you can learn to pause and mindfully notice the experiences you are having as an objective observer, and you can start deciding which thought trains you want to jump on. Once you clear out your painful experiences from the past and break out of old mental and emotional patterns, you can become a much more conscious caregiver.

CHAPTER FIVE

HOW TO MANAGE GUILT AND GRIEF

KAREN HOURTEVENKO

Karen Hourtevenko, Nurse Practitioner, Registered Psychotherapist, and Certified Master Coach, grapples with a promise that she made as a child to "take care of her mom." Sometimes, grappling with grief means letting go of old, impossible responsibilities.

J ust when I thought life was set, my world took an unexpected turn. Grief started early in my life. I remember as if it were yesterday, when both of my great-grandmothers, who were in their late nineties, passed. They were amazing yet different in personality. Both of them made an impact in my life. I remember seeing both not long before they passed as the family was called in to say final goodbyes. They lay in their beds in their individual homes, frail and tired, yet they smiled at each of us. I remember clearly our family going into their homes, waiting outside the bedroom door until each of us was asked to stand with them for one last time. I was only ten when my great-grandmother died. I can see her as if I was there right now. From what I recall, she was only about four-foot-ten and looked like Granny Clampet from *The Beverly Hillbillies*. She was always kind. Her life was tough, as it was for so many of her era. Her husband passed earlier, and she had to raise her family alone. I stood in her room, waiting as my sister went up to see her. She talked to her, then it was my turn. As I walked closer, she smiled and said, "Karen, your job is to take care of your mother!"

I remember smiling and saying innocently, "Okay, Nan, I will take care of Mom." We all took our turn then left. Word came later that she had passed. She was a few months short of her hundredth birthday.

A few years later, my second great-grandmother's health was failing, so we made the trip to her house in a different part of Nova Scotia, and we did the same thing. She was a larger lady with a big laugh and dark hair, which was remarkable for someone her age. She always seemed strong. As with my other great-grandmother, we stood in line at the entrance to her room and went in one by one, oldest to youngest. As I walked up to her, she smiled and said, "Karen, your job is to take care of your mother."

I just smiled and said, "I will, Nan." Those words had more impact in my life than I realized. I smiled at both of them, because to me it seemed like a normal request. I was okay with helping my mom; I loved her!

After the passing of my second great-grandmother, my grandmother (her daughter) came to live with us. They had lived together for years; in fact, my grandmother took care of her, and now it was my mom's turn to take care of her own mother.

My grandmother lived with us for five years. She was a great addition to our family, and I spent a lot of time with her. Sadly, a few years after moving in with us, she developed bowel cancer. Treatment was on and off, yet she remained happy throughout it all. As the disease progressed, we knew she would not be with us much longer. We managed her as long as we could at home, Mom taking care of her and I spending time in her room, just talking and hanging by her side, doing my homework. She never complained. I knew since the age of twelve that I was going to be a nurse, so to me it seemed normal to be with her. She ended up in hospital for the last eight weeks of life. I was seventeen by then. I walked to the hospital each afternoon after school and sat with her until the end of visiting hours. My aunt or my mom would be there too. I would help her, providing what she needed, walking her to the bathroom, getting ice water, and talking, just spending time. Although she remained positive, I knew she was in pain. She loved to tell all the nursing staff, "This is my granddaughter, and she is going to be a nurse!"

I remember the loss I felt when she passed, but I also remember a sense of peace because I knew she was no longer in pain. She was a woman of strong faith; she kneeled and prayed every night and had no fear of dying because she felt she knew where she was going. We never really spoke about her death, yet we often laughed at Nana's quirks and Nana-isms. Mom never let on how much she missed her.

Our family was familiar with death because my dad was a minister, so funerals were a part of our lives. He and Mom faced death with calmness because they were confident that Heaven was a place for the living. Dad showed tears with things that touched him, and Mom was the quiet type.

By 2000, I was married with three children, my youngest a newborn. My mom was suffering from fatigue and bleeding that turned out to be uterine cancer. I remember the call when my world stopped! Her cancer was a type that had a limited life expectancy. I felt an emptiness and loss. The sadness that came over me was intense. I kept thinking, *What am I going to do? I am not ready to lose my Mom. I have three young children, I need her.*

Denial is a normal part of any illness, I know that, yet no one can understand it until you are there. Denial is like the ostrich: if your head is in the ground, you don't have to see what is ahead. Her surgery date was set, and we were all there with her. It was just her uterus, I told myself. The surgery would be fast, and she would be fine. Four hours went by, there was no update, and it began to dawn on me that something was wrong. The longer time passed, my anxiety heightened, even though they told us the surgery was extended because they were waiting for the pathology lab to confirm or deny cancer. Results later confirmed it was not only cancer but also "clear cell carcinoma," a fast-growing cancer with no proven successful chemotherapy treatment. Recommendations included radiation and a study drug, to which she agreed.

YOU CAN CARE FROM FAR AWAY

Over the next few months, I went through a roller coaster of emotions as I struggled with worry and the distance between us and questioned how I could take care of her, being so far away. I wanted to be there and make sure she was okay. I *needed* to be there. After all, I was the nurse in the family! Over the next few months, I travelled back and forth with all three kids in tow and other times alone so that I could take care of Mom. My siblings were there in the same province, and of course my dad was there too, yet I felt I was the one they looked to for advice. I felt helpless and hopeless at times, looking for other options or treatments to save her. The eight-month journey was difficult for us all, and all the while, Mom never complained, or at least not to her family. She was a quiet, strong lady who only shared her thoughts or feelings when she really needed to, and when she did, we listened. She was clear with what she wanted: no chemo treatment if the study drug didn't work, because she was told it would not work, and she didn't want to lose her hair; and she wanted to stay at home as long as she could, provided we could take care of her there. There were no other demands or expectations.

Mom and Dad had a small home on the lake on the outskirts of Halifax — it was our family cottage when we were kids. We moved around as a family, so we never had a home of our own, except for the cottage. Mom loved it there; the lake was calm, and her creative skills were apparent in her flower gardens on the property. She wanted to live there after retirement and enjoy life with Dad.

I felt an overwhelming sense of guilt. I was in Ontario, and my parents and my siblings were across the country. How could I possibly be in both places at the same time? The words of my great-grandmothers rang in my ears over and over again: *Karen, it is your job to take care of your mother!* I realized that my guilt ran deeper than I thought. How could I have promised such a thing then move to Ontario fifteen years later? I struggled with that during her illness and afterward. It created such a pain in my heart. I was logical in my thinking: I could not just move back, yet I wanted to be there with her.

When my sister or I couldn't be there, my dad took on the caregiver role, and when we were there, he stepped back. My siblings were there as often as they could as well. None of us were geographically close. I managed issues with health-care providers by phone when I was asked. I sought out other treatment options to try to save her, because that was my job — or so I thought. Life carried on. It was a more difficult life for all of us, especially for Mom.

EMBRACE DENIAL

During those difficult months, I think we were all in denial. There was no way this could happen; after all, Mom was always there, guiding us quietly, keeping the family strong. How could this be our reality? A reality where she would not be with us. Over the course of her illness, she was fortunate enough to have an amazing general practitioner, Dr. Aiden Carey, who became our angel and lifeline for our family. She had a team at the Queen Elizabeth II Hospital in Halifax, so we knew she was getting the best care.

Many people go through denial when there is an illness, and reactions can manifest differently than others. Dad had his role: taking her to appointments, running errands, getting her out and yes, avoiding the enviable when he could. Dad had an amazing way of not dealing with his emotions because he was a minister. He was supposed to help others, so therefore he should be able to keep it together. When it came to me, I had three small kids at home, one of which was a newborn. I struggled to accept that my mom would not be there to see my kids grow up. I also struggled not being in Nova Scotia for her and leaving my family behind in Ontario. She loved her grandchildren, yet she was struggling to live, and she too realized she wouldn't see them grow. As a young mom at the time, I could not imagine not calling my mom for advice. What would I do, how would I survive?

HOW TO HOPE

My mom received radiation treatment and also took the study drug, while travelling back and forth to her oncologist for updates. In our last visit, we sat in the examination room together at the hospital clinic. Her oncologist sat on one side of the exam table, and Mom sat in a chair. He was holding her chart and with a slight glance her way he said, "There is nothing more we can do." The room fell silent.

A moment later she responded. "You have just given me my death sentence." I knew those words had huge meaning. He took any hope she had away. And with that I saw her give up.

I was so angry with the oncologist. While I understand prognosis and being transparent with patients, I also knew that having hope can be the difference between life and death. No one has the right to take away a person's hope, yet this logical and unemotional oncologist did just that. He shared the news as if he were talking about the weather. In my career, I have spent hours with patients, including those who were dying. I always gave them hope. Regardless of the reality, when the physician gives up, so does the patient, unless the person has the ability to fight. I was broken, disheartened, and dismayed at the lack of caring.

One month after this appointment, I was home again. I received a call from my sister informing me that Mom was in hospital, that her bowel was obstructed, and they were going to let her die. I was distraught. I had to get there to say goodbye. I was able to get a plane ticket to Halifax that day. Thankfully, when I arrived she was home and settled. The obstruction had opened up, and her pain was gone. We thought she was out of the dark, but the following morning, we were back in hospital. We sat in the emergency department and waited. The nurse told me that a surgeon was called. I was shocked when I saw a familiar face. He looked at me and asked, "What are you doing here?" I asked him the same.

Dr. Van Boxel was a surgeon my husband and I knew from Sudbury, Ontario. He had decided on a career change and had moved to Halifax. I told him that my mom was the patient and shared her story. He examined her and told me, "Typically we would treat her pain and assist her in her last days. Since she is young, I will remove the part of the bowel that is not working." And that he did. He gave us time ... he gave *her* time. I was never so happy to see a familiar face.

That surgery gave mom and our family another six weeks. We spent time with her and did what we had to do. Her general practitioner was amazing to her and our family. He is well known in the palliative care circle, and we are so grateful that he took on her care. When she could no longer travel in to see him, he came to her. He guided her care and allowed us the privilege to care for her at home, right until the end.

I returned to Ontario, getting things organized at work and for the family, knowing I would soon have to return east. Dr. Van Boxel called me personally two weeks after Mom was released from the hospital. I asked him if I should come back now. He said, no, not today. He told me she had a couple of weeks and no more than one month to live. I was so grateful for that call. I did what I had to do then and went back to Nova Scotia, kids in tow, with plans to stay there until the end. And that was what I did.

EASE THE BURDEN AND TALK ABOUT WORRIES

During her last weeks, I drove her to appointments and cleaned out clothes from closets that she had kept for years. And we talked about life, what she wanted and what she worried about. Mom's biggest worry was for Dad; she knew he would not do well without her. She also wanted to make quilts for all her grandchildren but would only be able finish half of them. She had selected specific patterns and designs. She asked me to make sure I completed that for my kids. I do hope someday I can fulfill her request.

Mom slept often in the last weeks. When she rested, I sat at her computer and wrote her obituary. I wanted it to be ready so I wouldn't forget important information. Dad wrote the funeral service, as he had done so many times before, but never for someone he loved so much.

A few days before Mom passed, she became very pensive. When I asked her what she was thinking about, she said, "Will you please build a granny flat on the side of your house and take care of your dad?" My heart stopped, and my mind took me back to my two great-grandmothers who told me that my job was to take care of my mom. It all became clear. That question was the cause of guilt I was experiencing. I told Mom not to worry about Dad, that he would be taken care of. But I knew I could not take on the responsibility of caring for him too; it would break me. She also told me that she always knew she would die from cancer. I was shocked. She never shared that fear with anyone.

COLLECT MEMORIES

During her final days, we made sure her grandchildren were around her. She loved them so much. She was known to them as "Mama" and "Grandma." My daughters asked her if they could paint her toenails, and she happily agreed, bright pink polish just like theirs. Her first pedicure was to be her last. That image of Mom in her chair, smiling while "her girls" gave her a pedicure, remains with me today. I treasure a picture I have of her from that day. As sick as she was in that photo, she beamed with pride as her granddaughters hugged her. She passed away a few days later at home, surrounded by her family, a friend, and her family doctor. She left this world in peace — I remember the distinct cry of a loon by the lake outside her window. The months that followed were difficult. She was young, only sixty-six years old, and it all seemed surreal. For years after Mom passed, I would remember something I wanted to tell or ask her, and I had to stop myself from picking up the phone to call her. Her voice was still on the answering machine at the house, and as much as I wanted to hear her again, it was too painful.

PRACTICE SELF-CARE

When things settle down, it is important to give yourself care. Do for yourself what you did for your loved one. Eat good food, exercise, talk when you need to, meditate, and do things to honour the person who is gone. Wallowing in the loss, the *I shoulda, coulda, woulda* does not bring them back. Be your own support system! Get up, dress up, show up each day, as if they were still alive. Ask yourself those hard questions:

1. Is holding on to this grief helping me or holding me back?
2. What advice would I give a friend if they were going through grief?
3. What positive impact did the person I lost have on me?

Here are my answers:

1. Grief was holding me back. I loved Christmas, and then I didn't. Now I do again. Techniques are required to assist the release of the emotional trauma of death. Find someone who can eliminate the negative emotion around death so you can live your best life.

2. If asked, I would tell a friend that even though it is okay to miss your loved one, you have a life to live, a purpose to fulfill, so live it well. Life is too short. Honour your loved one by honouring yourself.

3. Mom and Dad parented us with appropriate rules and guidance, which changed as we aged. Parenting evolved to mentoring in early childhood, to friendship as an adult. Mom taught me cooking, sewing, crafts, music, leadership, and wisdom. Dad taught me leadership, comforting the sick, and counselling. They taught me what a supportive and loving relationship was and the importance of family.

* * *

Being a caregiver can bring both blessings and curses. There is much to learn from life, and which story you attach to it will determine how you live. Look for the silver lining, and there will be calm even when there is pain.

CHAPTER SIX

HOLD ON TO THE ROLLER COASTER

BONNIE MULVIHILL

Bonnie Mulvihill, a reiki master, shares the ebb and flow of her nine-year caregiving journey. She emphasizes the benefits of having a life separate from her caregiving role and focuses on patience, a sense of humour, and optimism.

have chosen to share a very personal story with you today. My hope is that it resonates with your soul and reverberates within you an eternal joy that comes from loving and caring for the physical presence of another human being.

As I lovingly reflect on my nine-year caregiving journey with my mother, I realize that, although we are all likely going to be caregivers at some point in time, in some way, shape, or form, our journeys may possibly take us to places we never thought we could go.

The year was 1996. My mother, Mary Cecilia Ward Johnstone, came to live with us at the tender age of eighty-six. I was forty-six. Our youngest son, Shawn, was nineteen and just about ready to leave the nest. Our oldest daughter, Lauralee, and oldest son, Scott, were already on their own. Greg, my husband of twenty-five years, and I were both working and easing into the awareness of an empty abode. Mother's presence was about to fill a void I didn't even realize existed. We cared for Mom for nine years until her passing on March 7, 2005. She was ninety-four years young, and this is our story.

My new caregiver journey began with a certain ring of trepidation. It was actually happening. My mom was coming to live with us. Suddenly, I realized that this was not the new progression of my life I had been anticipating. Now, instead of looking forward to an exciting new chapter, I was cast into a life of responsibility that I really wasn't sure I could handle. Being this type of caregiver was new to me. I wanted to run away and hide. I didn't think I would be able to withstand the worry that I felt brewing in my heart. Although my mother never believed that her health conditions were disabilities, the cold, hard fact was that she was eighty-six years old, legally blind, and hard of hearing. I knew this would pose several challenges.

Right up until she came to live with us, she lived in her own home and even had tenants. She was very independent. However, once she was taken out of her familiar environment where she had navigated with ease, things

70

changed drastically. She was no longer the carefree mom I had always known and identified with. She was completely dependent on *me* now. The heaviness of that weighed on me like an anchor holding its ship by a tethered rope to keep it from going adrift. I don't know if I was the ship or the rope, but I knew I didn't want to be tied down. I never had to look after my mom for one day in my life, and now here we were, face to face in an awkward, unpredictable situation.

The plan was never for Mom to live with us in her elderly years. My sister was a nurse and was exceptionally in tune with her unique rhythm. I, on the other hand, was not. Sadly, my sister died at the young age of forty-two in a car accident that also took the life of her fifteen-year-old son. Two other young men also lost their lives that tragic evening. My sister's husband was driving the van for the hockey team; they were on their way back from a tournament when the catastrophe occurred.

My mother's care now had to be put front and centre, while the silence of the grieving process played itself out in the not so silent background. My mother and I were strangers, in a way. She had lived her life on the East Coast, and I had lived mine with my family here in Ontario. I'd left when I was eighteen. We talked often on the phone but only actually visited once a year at the most. We were as close as a distant relationship permitted. My mother was someone I went to for guidance, advice, and "mom stuff," but she was not my closest buddy. I actually left home young to live life on my terms, free of rules and responsibilities. I wanted to marry and have children and live happily ever after. Yet here we were. *How can I possibly do this?* I asked myself. Some days it was more than I could bear. I cannot express to you the roller coaster of feelings. I was so frightened for her and so worried for me. How could I look after this woman who had cared for *me* my entire life? On one hand, I cried because I thought I couldn't do it, while on the other hand I cried because I didn't always want to. But I constantly prayed that I would get the time to become reacquainted with her in a deeper way.

FIND CREATIVE SOLUTIONS

In the beginning, we danced a very wobbly dance, but every time we came up against a new challenge as my mother aged, we also came up with new and creative solutions. When she couldn't find her way to the bathroom, we installed railings to guide her there. When she slipped in the hallway, we extended the railings so she was able to go unassisted into the living room to watch (listen to) TV. When she could no longer search out the things to prepare her own lunch, we did it together ahead of time to make it as stress-free as possible for her while still honouring her independence. But I was feeling the pressure. Although all of us chipped in to assist with her care, I knew that the full burden of it was on me. I wasn't sure how this would all work out or where we would go from there. And then she fell and broke her hip.

My mother was not a hospital person, and the thought of going somewhere strange again was not appealing to her. We did not know at the time that she had broken her hip. She did not want me to call the ambulance, assuring me that she was fine and just wanted to give it a little time to heal on its own. After twelve hours, I knew it had to be a lot more serious and persuaded her to make the trek to the hospital. The ambulance came, and a new journey began. The doctors said that a lot of people her age die after hip surgery. My immediate response was, "You obviously don't know my mother," and we changed doctors.

GET HOME CARE HELP

After surgery, my mother healed quite well, considering she was in her late eighties. The beautiful thing that came from this situation was that home care came home with us and stayed with Mom, a couple of hours a week, until her death in 2005. They were angels sent from Heaven. In the beginning it was difficult for Mom, who never had strangers care for her before, but within a short time she gathered them all under her wing. Most days, they laughed and joked and really enjoyed her company. It gave me the well-deserved respite that I needed. I knew if my mother was going to get the best care from me, I had to take good care of myself. My first step in that direction was taking advantage of the few free hours a week that became available to me through the home care program. I was also offered a palliative program, but that was just too overwhelming for me even to think about at the time. I knew my mom wanted to die at home, and I hoped I could honour that, but I wasn't ready to think about it. In retrospect, I wish I had been in the frame of mind at least to consider their offer. Near the end of our journey together, I was starting to burn out, and I now believe the palliative program could have boosted my mental health at such a stressful time in my life.

SEPARATE YOURSELF FROM YOUR CAREGIVER DUTIES

Looking after "me" became a priority when I realized I was becoming mentally and physically too exhausted to cope. I felt like there was no one on Earth who could look after my mom the way I could. It was turning into an obsession, consuming my mind day and night. With some help, I realized I needed some space. Even though it was difficult, in the end I made a conscious effort to continue my toastmaster classes and to slip away for an occasional weekend retreat with my hubby. I also made the effort to stay connected to my volunteer work in the community. Although it was not easy to separate myself from my caregiver duties, I knew for my own sanity I had to do it. I loved my mother so much that if I did not stay alert to where her feelings ended and mine started, I would be in trouble. I came to a point where I wasn't sure any more if I was feeling her pain or my own, and that is a scary thing to be in constant mental anguish. I was scared and exhausted. She was old and tired and perhaps leery of what lay ahead on the physical plane. This was not healthy, so I cherished the wee bit of time I had away to keep a healthy perspective.

I also attended yoga classes, and it is only now that I realize how very healing that physical movement was. It gave me expanded energy for my tired body, rest for my busy mind, and solace for my soul. Another little mission I partook of during my caregiving reprieves was volunteering with therapeutic horseback riding, an amazing program designed to build a bond between horses and children with disabilities. I had the incredible experience of side-walking with the children on horseback, feeling their excitement as they connected with the animal whose quiet, calm energy had such a health-giving effect on them (and me). I witnessed a sometimes highly charged energy transform into a peaceful, relaxed, happy child having fun. Being out in the fresh air and mobile was invigorating for me as well. I loved it. One of the most dynamic things I did on my little respites was to join a toastmaster club. I was absolutely terrified to speak in public, but my desire to tell my story was stronger than my fear of being vulnerable. I was encouraged to write my speeches and then present them at the meetings. I found both endeavours cathartic. It offered me another avenue to express my feelings, both in the writing and in the speaking.

I often wonder whether I would have even pursued (and grown exponentially from) any of my volunteer opportunities had I not looked to outside adventures for stress relief. Life has a beautiful way of looking after us, doesn't it?

Mom and I communicated very well, but I am sure that there were days when she was as tired of receiving as I was of giving, so the change of pace was good for her too. My little absences provided Mom with the opportunity to talk to someone other than me. I suppose it was, seemingly, a welcomed departure from the repetitiveness of her preemptive thoughts of, *Am I becoming a burden? How will you get along without me? Where am I going? What is it like to die?*

MAINTAIN EMOTIONAL AND PHYSICAL CONNECTION

Another challenge I faced as a caregiver and a loving daughter was to make sure Mom never became isolated. She was always so particular about how she dressed. It was difficult for me when she didn't want to get dressed up any more. She was a lady who, well into her eighties, always wore a skirt, nylons, and high heels. It was sad for me when she accepted the track pants and slippers I offered her. Then there came a point in time where she didn't have the desire to get dressed at all any more. Mom at the table in a nightgown and housecoat was something I had never witnessed in my entire life. She did, however, consent to wear the pretty nightgowns and robes to dine in. Her not coming to the table was never an option; how she could sit with us in her own dignified, graceful manner became the focus. Gradually, her balance and sense of direction waned. For a person who was legally blind, this was perilous. Things as simple as using a fork to eat became difficult. Searching to find the food on the plate and then struggling to create a momentum from plate to mouth also became a tedious task. Carole, our daughter-in-law, would sometimes quietly move Mom's food just to the end of her fork so she would feel the sweet taste of success. Later, I would cut her food in proper proportions so that eating with her fingers was not so cumbersome.

Nevertheless, Mother's conversations were so enlightening that no one even noticed that, on occasion, this elegant lady ate with her fingers. Perhaps she felt emotionally isolated at times, dealing with her own aging and the changes in her life, but there was no physical isolation. She was surrounded by love and lots of social interaction.

Although caring for Mom was sometimes overwhelming with all the setbacks, the decline in health and the increased dependency, working with the positives, was always a sustaining factor for us. We were so blessed with patience, a sense of humour, an optimistic attitude, and an unwavering trust in the unknown. I think had it not been for the grace of each of these blessings, the accumulation of disappointments and heartbreak might have been insurmountable. The good times were many, but oh, the disappointments when another factor of decline reared its head, and oh, the heartbreak when the inevitable death process itself began.

ACCEPT WHAT IS AND LIVE IN THE NOW

Another magical gift I learned from my caregiving experience is acceptance of what is. Living in the NOW helped me tremendously to stay focused and centred on the task at hand. As each new setback developed, we accepted, we cried, we prayed, and we moved on. Acceptance turned into gratitude, and gratitude turned into hope and healing in that moment. Since Mom was in her mid-nineties, hope was not a long-term goal, but we enjoyed its stimulating energy in the moment. My mother saw humour in almost everything, and it sure helped when things were not so funny. I remember being asked if it was hard to deal with criticism, frustration, or anger from her. Honestly, I was so tired that I don't think I could have dealt with one ounce of criticism. I did, on occasion, misinterpret her feedback or guidance as criticisms due to my own frustration or impatience. Mom was very cognizant of my feelings. I, on the other hand, was not always as accommodating.

STAY OBJECTIVE

It's sort of an oxymoron that becoming so close to someone can make you complacent in a sense, and much less objective. It's that fuzzy barrier I was referring to earlier where it's not clear who is feeling what. For example, it's time for Mom's shower. I am feeling rushed and overwhelmed, with so many things to do in such a short time. Perhaps she is feeling bossed around, rushed, tired, sore, and maybe dependent and cantankerous. Or was that me? Anger? I never saw my mother angry. I think at times I would have welcomed her anger instead of her quietude, or perhaps disappointment, when I responded with my own frustrating comments as the pain began to seep through the foundation. I know now that I did the best I could with the tools I had at the time, and no matter what transpired, my mother loved me through it all.

ACCEPT CARE RECIPIENT RESISTANCE

Another thing I muddled through was dealing with Mom's resistance from time to time. Care recipient resistance is not unusual. I can honestly say that I really did see her resistance as a last-ditch effort to maintain some semblance of control. She was quite the authoritarian in her day. Even in her late eighties, she would have me get the "manager" on the phone; no one of a lesser position would do, even if the task was quite menial. I empathized with the poor clerk who waited on her in the shoe store. I did not know that there were so many ways to accommodate your customer! And in the restaurant, the server had better not have anyone else to wait on while they assured Mother that her order was to be prepared exactly to her preference. It was actually enjoyable to see her feistiness. She was essentially quite gentle and congenial, but she would always say "business is business." She came into her own when she was vying for impeccable service. I could see that she was quite enjoying her last little practice of sovereignty. I was given the grace to act like it was all normal and was blessed with an amazing sense of patience because of it.

Seeing the lighter side of her resistance is fun to recollect, the darker side not so much. Mom's everyday normal routine consisted of her going into the bathroom and having her soothing shower. The anxiety in me rises as I remember her poignantly stating that she would no longer be physically going into the bathroom for her bath or shower. The caregiver in me understood; the daughter did not. I did everything in my power to outtalk her, to reason with her, compromise with her, and even beg her to get up and get in that shower. Even as I write this, I feel that sense of panic. She was ninety-four. Somehow, I knew that this was the beginning of the end, and if getting her into that shower meant I could keep her longer, I was not going to quit trying. I now know that was wrong. I lost my sense of objectivity. I just wanted her to get in the damn shower so everything would stay the same.

Change is a scary thing when you are losing someone you love. I think her resistance to the bath was the most difficult waters I had to navigate as a caregiver, because deep down, I knew death was approaching. The tethered cord that had always bound us together was about to be severed. The ship was preparing for her final voyage, and we both had no idea where she was going. I cried, I prayed, and I moved on to the next hurdle. Consequently, when I accepted that she was too weak to get into the shower, everything changed. She really delighted in the quiet, unstructured tempo of sponge bathing in solitude in her own bedroom. After she was bathed, I loved to put cream on her back and her little feet. We enjoyed the simple, natural time spent together. We flowed into a new ceremonial rhythm, all without the chaos of the bathroom routine. Once again, acceptance prevailed.

PUT YOURSELF IN YOUR LOVED ONE'S SHOES

I never really worried that my mom was not in control of her own destiny. Even into her nineties, she would remind us that she could still get on a train and move to my brothers' to live if she was too much of a "bother." You had to love her vigour and sense of adventure!

I wish I had the understanding then that I have now regarding the physiological, psychological, emotional, and social changes one goes through as one ages and breathes into the dying process. I used to think that she was just pushing my buttons to get her own way at times, because as the end became perceptible, she did not want to be alone for one minute. I began to feel so trapped that I dared not even go to the store, for coffee, or, God forbid, have a luxurious bath. I felt my freedom draining from my soul. I did not understand that she was anticipating her own departure and that she did not want to die alone. I often responded to her apprehension with my own anxiety. I did not take the time to put myself in her shoes and feel what it must be like to lose my independence, to feel my earthly existence slipping away. As a loving daughter/caregiver, I did not have the mental fortitude to put myself in her shoes because I just could not go there. However, I could love her with all my heart and be present for her until it was time for her ship to sail.

At the age of ninety-four, my mother died very peacefully in her own bed at home with us on March 7, 2005, surrounded by love. My caregiving journey with her had come to a very tranquil end. The ship has sailed, untethered and free. I would not trade one moment of it.

Ironically, starting over *without* my mother propelled me backward on the same shaky ground that I had started out *with* her nine years earlier. After my mother passed, I sensed a myriad of emotions. Immediately, I felt a tremendous lack of confidence. It was as if someone had pulled a platform out from under me. I felt all alone and on unfamiliar ground. I no longer had my rock. I was floating again in unchartered waters, now without a captain.

I did not feel anger, guilt, or even sorrow right away. I felt a tremendous sense of relief that she was finally home safe. I sensed that she could see clearly now and walk, talk, sing, and be joyfully independent again. I felt peaceful knowing that I had held her hand as she left this world. My mother prayed for a peaceful death her whole life and I felt that, by the grace of God, she did have precisely that. I felt a deep sense of freedom for us both. I no longer had to worry about her choking on her food or falling down and breaking a limb or having a stroke. I felt free to carry on with my life as I had known it before she came to live with us. I knew I would never see her physical presence on Earth again, but I know that she is always with me in a very sacred, spiritual way. On the morning of her funeral, I was writing her eulogy, and our youngest son Shawn gave me an angel with wings holding a butterfly. That said it all.

Mother's last words will always echo in my memory. *"I don't know where I am going, but I will love you from wherever I am!"*

My story ends with a favourite poem of mine that stems from a piece of advice that my dear, dying mother gave to me. I encourage each and every living soul to share the talents that they are born with to create more peace, more love, and more harmony in this extraordinary world that we live in.

THE SHIP OF LIFE
John T. Baker, 1917–2006
Based on Henry Van Dyke's "The Parable of Immortality"

Along the shore I spy a ship
As she sets out to sea;
She spreads her sails and sniffs the breeze
And slips away from me.
I watch her fading image shrink,
As she moves on and on,
Until at last she's but a speck,
Then someone says, "She's gone."
Gone where? Gone only from our sight
And from our farewell cries;
That ship will somewhere reappear
To other eager eyes.
Beyond the dim horizon's rim
Resound the welcome drums,
And while we're crying, "There she goes!"
They're shouting, "Here she comes!"
We're built to cruise for but a while
Upon this trackless sea
Until one day we sail away
Vanishing into infinity.

CHAPTER SEVEN

THE DIFFERING CULTURES OF DYING

WENDY HILL

Wendy Hill, Indigenous Spiritual Healer, provides a spiritual take on caregiving and shares how her dreams changed her perspective, which helped her prepare for her role as a caregiver.

My story begins with a dream. My father is walking toward me. He looks very pale, unsteady, and scared, which my father was not. He was my hero, protector, provider, a man who could be as playful as a five-year-old child and as strong as a nine-foot-tall bodyguard. His name was Ron and he was a Mohawk, dark-skinned, very fit. He worked hard all his life as an ironworker. He took pride in his identity as a Native man and a father of eight. When my mother died from stomach cancer fifteen years earlier, he was heartbroken and remained in a deep depression for five years.

He eventually did recover but never dated or remarried. We only had a few weeks to prepare for her death, since her illness was not detected until she went for gallbladder surgery. We got the unexpected news of her cancer and her impending death all at the same time. It was too late for treatment. At the time, I was eight months pregnant and couldn't wait to share my baby with her. She was an awesome mother who loved and nurtured all eight of us children. She had no favourites and treated us equally. My father was the same. They were both hard workers and taught us to work hard for a living and to value our children and family. I was working at the time but would soon be going on maternity leave, and I wanted to spend every day with her before she left the physical world. I wanted to give back to her the way she gave to us. I wanted to feed her, help her to the bathroom, bathe her, and take care of her in her final days. I just loved her so much and wanted to help her however I could. I hoped she would live longer, but before having my baby and before my maternity leave even started, I got the call.

I was on my way to work on April 11, 1996. When I was told of her death, I pulled off onto the side of the road and cried. And cried. And cried. I was devastated. I don't know how long I stayed there, but once I managed to pull myself together, I turned the van around and headed home. I didn't want to see my family, because I knew it was going to be hard, especially to see my father. He was so broken, weak, and sad. The wind had been taken out of his sails. As time went on, we helped him get through this very difficult period and eventually healed as a family, but it wasn't easy.

A few weeks after my mother's death, she came to me in a dream and told me not to be sad or guilty because I wasn't there when she passed away. She told me that she left when she did because the people who were there in the room with her were strong enough and could handle her death. My father had left the room to smoke, and during his five-minute absence, she died. He was so upset that he wasn't there for her, but she wanted me to tell him that she chose to die when he left the room because she knew he couldn't handle her dying in front of him. She said it would've been too difficult on her, as well, to leave with me or my father in the room, so she left when we weren't there. She said everyone gets to decide who will be there when they die. I felt relieved and shared my dream with my dad. We both felt some peace in her message.

When I had the dream of my father looking frail, pale, and unsteady, I walked toward him in the dream, and as we reached each other, he collapsed into my arms. I stood him up to steady him and noticed that he was ice-cold. I started to rub his back and his arms to warm his body. I asked him why he was so cold. He said, "I'm dying, and I'm scared."

I was shocked! My strong, protective father felt like a weak, small man in my arms. It made me very sad that he was no longer this strong protector but now someone who was weak and in need of my help. I asked, "What are you afraid of? Just think, you will see Mom again and your parents and grandparents and your sisters, and there are so many looking forward to seeing you."

He said, "Do you think that's where I'm going?"

I said, "Yes!" without any hesitation.

He continued, "I wasn't always there for you kids, and I gambled."

I said, "You weren't here because you were away working for us kids. You always came home and shared your money with us. You didn't beat us or leave us. You were a good father, and yes, that's where you're going!"

He said, "Keep talking."

"Well, you won't have any bills to worry about, and you won't have any more pain. It will be a great time and a great celebration."

Then he took his last breath and died in my arms. I cried so hard, I woke up crying as if it had really happened. I continued to cry for two days. I couldn't leave my home or go anywhere. After two days of crying, I accepted that my father was going to die and that he was going to be with me to die. I knew that I was going to be the one to help him in that time. I had to prepare myself. I started visiting him often, as much as possible. I didn't want to have any regrets of missing time or knowledge that he wanted to pass on.

A few months after I had this telling dream, he informed me that health inspectors found mould in his house, and he had to move out. It was everywhere, so they would be tearing the house down. I told him he could move in with me until he was able to figure out what he wanted to do. At first he refused because he didn't want to be a burden, but then one day he showed up at my doorstep carrying his clean socks and said, "I'm moving in!"

TALK ABOUT IT

When I saw him come through the door, I realized he looked just like he had in my dream. I quickly turned away from him so he wouldn't see the tears rolling down my cheeks. I guided him to his room, and we began our time together. I took the rest of the summer off to be with him. I cooked his favourite meals, took him to casinos, and did whatever he wanted to do. Then, after three months or so, I noticed that he was talking about dying more often. I tried to discourage him and told him how he would have a new house soon and would be able to enjoy it. One day, when he was talking about death, a voice told me to let him talk, so I did. Then I asked him if he wanted to hear a dream I had about him. He said, "Sure," so I told him my dream. It got uncomfortably quiet. I looked over at him as we sat out on the porch looking out toward the road. He had tears in his eyes, so I asked him, "What brings your tears?"

He answered, "I guess I needed to hear that you thought I was a good dad."

I cried too and said, "Of course." We continued to sit outside and visit and drink our coffee on that beautiful summer morning.

A few weeks later, I started to find tissues with blood on them in his room; he had a nasty cough. I insisted he go see his doctor and get his lungs checked. My father had smoked since he was twelve years old, when he started working and was able to buy his own cigarettes. About that time, I had also noticed that he had started to slow down in his activities. He was still driving his truck, carrying water bottles to my cooler, but he was much slower. A few weeks after he saw the doctor, all of his activities stopped. He had bronchitis and was on medication. He wasn't doing well. A month later, we found out he had lung cancer, which had already spread to his liver, kidneys, and brain. He had been complaining of headaches and was taking a lot of Tylenol. When we found out about the cancer diagnosis, the doctors gave him two days to live if he went home. He lasted a week.

CELEBRATE LIFE

His dying days were sad, but they were celebratory days as well. He wasn't in a lot of pain — cancer had gone to his brain and was somehow shutting down the pain receptors. He continued to smoke, which made him happy, and he could still eat. So, every day we had a houseful of people wanting to visit him and cook for him and do whatever they could for him. I was just trying my best not to cry in front of him. He asked me to be strong for him. He said I could cry when he was gone. But I cried anyway, in the shower, in my car, and whenever I had a private moment. My sadness ran deep, but I made sure he was happy and comfortable and that his visitors felt welcome. These are the teachings my family taught us — to be welcoming and inviting. Even though I knew the day would come soon, I was dreading it. Luckily, my dad seemed happy to die. He talked about how his relatives would react and greet him. His happiness to be reunited with my mom and our relatives was a relief to all of us. He was able to talk and visit up until the night before he died.

It was a Friday night, and my husband had just returned from an iron-workers' camp job he had been employed at for a few years. He worked two weeks straight and then had two weeks off work. My dad loved my husband and really liked visiting with him. My father kept asking for him and wondering when Mike would return. I told my husband that my father had been sleeping the whole day and was hardly getting up, and that he'd stopped eating. I urged Mike to go in his bedroom anyway, at least to say hi. So he went into the room, where there were about twenty family members sitting around visiting with him and with each other. Everyone got quiet, and I told my dad, "Mike is here now." He turned his head and nodded to acknowledge him. I knew my dad was waiting for him to get home to comfort me.

OFFER REASSURANCE

We had grown so close over the past six months that he lived with us, and I was so sad to see his life leaving him. I needed someone there to be strong for me. Mike was there now, and I sensed my father's relief. Although I needed Mike's strength, I had tried very hard to keep busy and to reassure my daughters and grandchildren that this was a process and that their grandfather would be happier with my mom and his parents and with our family in the spirit world. Our Native teachings tell us that however we handle death, we are teaching our children and family how to handle our own death. Because I had the experience of losing my mother, I knew it would be difficult on my father if I wasn't okay with his passing. I wanted to be okay with it, and in the end, I was the one who sat with him on his last day here on Earth. I held his hand and told him how he had done his job well. I reminded him how his eight children were all grown up and had our own families and that we were okay. I told him he didn't need to worry about us. I told him I didn't want to move from my home if he died there. There was a time a few months earlier that I thought he was dead in his bed, and I freaked out. I came into his bedroom, and there he lay looking like he was dead. I yelled, "DAD!!!!!" He jumped up, scared, and we both laughed. I told him, "I thought you were dead! Oh MY God, you better not die at my house! I will be traumatized! I will have to move from here." I was pretty shook up, but we were able to laugh afterward. But I knew this was still bothering him and part of the reason why he didn't want to die. So I reassured him that I would be all right and that I would not move from my house if he chose to die there.

After I said those words, he looked like he was going to reply; his eyes were shut, but his mouth moved slightly. It even looked like he might sit right up. Then he exhaled a long breath, smiled, and then he died. I waited for him to breathe. His breath didn't come. Seconds seemed like minutes. I was in shock. Maybe four or five minutes passed, and I left the bedroom and went toward my siblings in the living room. I said, "I think Dad just died!" My younger brother went running into his room, and just then my dad took another breath, very short, then my brother said to get his sister, my aunt. I went into the living room and got her. My auntie went into his room and he breathed again, very short. We all waited for about ten minutes, and he didn't breathe again. I didn't cry or feel any great sadness. I was relieved for him, for he was no longer lonely and sick.

MAKE THE WORLD A BETTER PLACE

Our teachings are very comforting, and as Native people, we believe that the body is meant to go back into the earth in a healthy way. Our body is only loaned to us for use while we are on this earth, and we have a responsibility to take care of it as it belongs to the Creator. When we are done the job we are meant to do here, we die. The family's responsibility is to take care of the body, to clean it, dress it with our traditional clothes, and sing our traditional songs to help the person's spirit leave the Earth. Our whole family and community come together to help with this process to send our people off in a respectful and honouring way, regardless of how they lived their life. This process helps everyone, and those who never got to say their goodbyes can say these things to the family or friends who come around for those ten days. I know that the ones who die don't want anyone to have hard feelings toward them or to be having a difficult time with their death. I had many dreams of the ones who died telling me to go on and to be happy and to not let their death ruin my life. To honour a person's life is to acknowledge the positive attributes of that person and to use their positivity to affect your own life in a good way. For instance, I had a niece who died from a fall down the stairs into a basement. She hit her head on the concrete floor and died instantly. She was only thirty-two, but her personality was so bubbly that she taught us to be happy and enjoy life because you just never know when it will be your day to go. She definitely lived life on her terms and tried her best not to hurt or harm others. Even though she was offended and hurt by different people in her life, she would just say, "I'm not going to let that bother me. The sun is shining for me too, and I'm going to enjoy my day!"

In my culture we have many teachings around how to handle death and dying from a healthy perspective, and it is almost an obligation to be okay after a death. My boyfriend actually came to me in a dream and said, "We are given life to be happy and enjoy our lives. You're not. You're angry and sad because of me and my death. I need you to be happy. It is bothering me that you're not happy or enjoying your life, and I know it's because of me." He told me how hard it is for him to be at peace when I'm crying and so sad because of him. He went on to say, "Did you ever hurt someone and know that this person is crying because of you and you can't apologize or comfort them?" He said it's not easy to be enjoying the spirit world when loved ones are miserable on the Earth. So, he said, "Every day you have here, you get to make all the choices to be enjoying life and you're not enjoying yourself."

We believe that the Creator asks us these two questions when we die: "Did you enjoy this life I gave you? And if not, why not? You have to make choices every day to enjoy your day." The other question he asks is, "How is the world a better place because you were there? What did you do to make it better?"

I learned so much through the deaths of my loved ones about how to live and how to die. It has been my blessing to be part of these peoples' lives and part of my loved ones' journey as they went onto the spirit world. I look at my life every day and say to myself, "If this were my last day on Earth, did I enjoy myself? And did I do something positive to help the world to be a better place?" The bottom line is, if you ever get a chance to be there for someone in their dying days (or in their living days), take it and make the most of it. It is a blessing and an honour to help someone transfer into the spirit world. The blessings that you receive are really tenfold, as they say, but you must do it for the right reasons, and if it's only to make their last days here as comfortable as possible, blessings to you.

CHAPTER EIGHT

WHEN YOU NEAR THE END: PALLIATIVE CARE

SANDI EMDIN

Sandi Emdin, registered social services worker, shares several inspiring stories about her real-life experiences caring for her vulnerable end-of-life patients. Her insights ease the way.

haven't thought about or written about my experience as a palliative care volunteer in a very long time. Thinking about it now brings back many memories. The experience changed my life, my path, and my purpose.

The year was 2001. I was a stay-at-home mom at the time, and finally, both my kids were settled into school all day. Before having kids, I was a social worker, and I was exploring the idea of returning to work. While checking the classifieds one day, I saw an advertisement recruiting palliative care volunteers. It described the position, the requirements, and the intensive training program that successful applicants would have to complete prior to being matched with clients. The training program was thirty hours and scheduled over two weeks. It started with an all-weekend intensive session and then a few evenings a week for two weeks. After being out of the workforce for several years, I thought this would be a great segue back in; a way to use my social work experience, connect with other professionals, and learn about my community. I was relatively new to Sudbury, Ontario, at that time. As I write this, I am embarrassingly aware of what I was thinking of back then when I was filling out my application: *What's in this for me?* How would this certification look on my resume? Would I meet someone at the training who was hiring? Selfishly, part of me was also thinking of how refreshing it would be not to have to be part of the homework, bath-time, and story-time routine at home. I was desperate for some adult time and eager to learn something new. So I signed up, I got in, and this is where my story begins.

RECOGNIZE THE POWER OF HUMAN CONNECTION

I don't think any of us in the class knew what we were getting into on that first day. We were a group of about fifteen of all ages and backgrounds, mostly strangers to each other. The facilitator handed everyone a thick binder, complete with section dividers, documents to be signed, the course outline, and our schedule. I was excited and ready to learn. Then she asked us to put our binders aside and told us to take turns introducing ourselves and share why we wanted to become a palliative care volunteer. Everyone's reason was different, and through that exercise we learned a lot about each other. For the next three days, we talked about our experiences with death, dying, and caregiving. We got to know each other by sharing our stories of love and loss, life and death, and heartaches and healing. It was an experience of very intimate bonding, very quick and very deep. For some of us, it was the first time we had shared our stories of loss out loud, and for others it had been many years since they'd talked about it. Yet it was in the sharing with one another that we were able to empathize and support one another. We listened, we felt, we wept, we hugged, we bonded, and we were reminded that we were not alone. It was something I'd never experienced before; this level of sharing — so raw, so real, and so safe. We didn't know it, but we were learning to create and hold the space for each other, which is arguably the most important skill for any caregiver.

As the training progressed, we learned about policies and procedures, ethics and confidentiality, and the importance of debriefing and self-care. This work was "heart" work, and we were going to need a lot of support to do it well. Much of the training was experiential as we practiced transfer-ring patients from a bed to a chair, lifting postures, toileting, and feeding. That's where a few of us, me included, started to really see first-hand how vulnerable our clients could be. To help us grasp the experience, the trainer had us take turns feeding each other in a hospital bed. It felt awkward spoon-feeding a virtual stranger in a hospital bed. I was giddy at first, finding it hard to get into the role. When it was my turn to be the patient and let my partner feed me a bowl of cereal by the spoonful ... woo! For the first time in the training, I had a glimpse of what it might feel like, on this side, to be vulnerable, helpless, and at the mercy of others for your care. I remember fighting to hold back tears, because for just a moment I felt like I was actually the patient. My role partner was focused, patient, her voice so gentle. It felt like there was just the two of us having this moment. And yet the room was filled with at least ten other people going through the same exercise. She spoke very little except to ask if I was okay, if I would like another spoonful, or if she was going too fast. The whole experience lasted only minutes, but all these years later I can still feel her presence in that moment. I'm tearing up as I write this as I am reminded of the power of human connection and to be truly seen by another person.

BE THERE AND HOLD THE SPACE

An integral part of the training was to attend a memorial service, organized just for our group, complete with flowers, music, prayer, coffee, and snacks following the service. After that, we spent the entire afternoon debriefing the memorial experience. As volunteers, we would need to be prepared to attend the services of our clients if they requested. Once again, we got to experience, feel, and share our stories of funerals, memorials, and other rituals connected to death. I had never witnessed that level of listening or felt the power in being heard. It truly was another example of how we were learning to be caregivers by taking care of each other and ourselves. We held the space for one another just by being there, being quiet, and listening; a powerful lesson.

PRACTICE GRATITUDE

When I signed up for the caregiving training, I didn't realize how much I would learn about myself. I expected to learn about how to take care of someone who was dying. But that was only one of the many teachings I received. Being immersed in the topics of death, dying, and caregiving, sharing personal experiences, and the bonding that happened was something I had never experienced before. Death awareness had awakened me of the certainty of death, but also to the preciousness of life. This death awareness had somehow snapped me out of taking my life for granted.

On the rides home after training, I remember feeling grateful to be alive and thinking, over and over, "Thank you." I'd be thinking of how grateful I was to be healthy, to have a healthy husband, and healthy kids; how lucky I was to be a stay-at-home mom. This shift in thinking was new for me. I would have been much more likely at the time to be complaining about the kids, my husband, or serious matters like having only one car. This new practice, new mindset, new attitude of gratitude, somehow left me feeling more joyful, more appreciative, and somehow lighter.

When I first started this gratitude practice over twenty years ago, I had a hard time coming up with just a few things to be grateful for, but now I can go on and on until I'm out of breath. It feels amazing every time. This lesson really changed my life. I learned when you feel grateful for what you have, you feel more happiness and joy. Up until then, I thought it was the other way around. I now practice thoughts of gratitude every day; when I first open my eyes, when I'm in the shower, at a traffic light, while I am cooking. It changes everything. Practicing a state of gratitude required more self-awareness than I was used to, yet so many gifts came from it. Ironically, this new awareness and gratitude for the gift of life came from weeks of talking about death. I had this new feeling of aliveness. I started to notice how much I complained, so I tried to count my blessings instead of the things I had to do when I got home. My usual mindset went something like this: "I have to pick up the kids, I have to get groceries, I have to gas up the car, I have to, I have to, I have to." This was not only exhausting, but it also sucked all the joy out of my day because I was focused on all the things I had to do. My mindset started shifting from thinking about all the things I had to do to the things I "got to do," because I could. I was alive. I was healthy. I still had time and energy to do things. It was only a minor shift in words yet such a major shift in thinking and feeling. I started thinking, I "get to" pick up the kids because I HAVE kids; I "get to" go grocery shopping because I have a car, money, and a family I love to feed. I "get to" cut the grass because I have a lawnmower and I know how to work it. This change in mindset was a seemingly small shift in thinking, yet it created a huge shift in the way I feel, keeping me in a daily state of gratitude for being alive.

Many years later, I spoke about this change in mindset in a TEDx talk titled "3 Small Words" (2014 Nickel City). TED talks are based on ideas worth spreading, and by then I had learned that sharing my idea could help others become aware of their mindset and help them create a new one using three small words like "I get to."

TAKE THREE DEEP BREATHS

Another "three small words" phrase that I love is "three deep breaths." This is one of the most useful practices I have ever encountered. It was introduced to me in the palliative care caregiver training as a strategy to be more present and to use your breath to focus and clear your mind. As volunteers, we were encouraged to practice taking three deep breaths before we met with clients in their home or in the hospital. The purpose was to help us get centred, focused, and into the present moment, because this work required active listening and our full attention. We practiced this technique of taking three deep breaths often during our training. I found it very difficult to think of nothing. Learning to focus on my breath by repeating, "breathe in, breathe out," helped. Sometimes I would repeat in my head, "I am here. Be here now," or "I am aware," over and over again. Remarkably, it worked. I felt calmer and more focused. I didn't know it then, but practicing three deep breaths would eventually lead me to practicing mindfulness and meditation several years later.

WALK TO REFRESH YOUR BODY, MIND, AND SPIRIT

Luckily for me, I have always been a walker. No matter where I've lived, I've always mapped out a walking route that takes about an hour and then walked that route everyday as part of my routine. Over the years, my walking routine helped me to relax, stay in shape, connect with a friend, or listen to my favourite music turned up loud. Later, my walking routine included the family dog. Oh, sure, we would take turns for a while, and we'd even walk her as a family now and then, but when push came to shove, I would be the one leashing her up. For a long time, I thought of "walking the dog" as one more thing I had to do. But things changed when I shifted from "I have to" walk the dog to I "get to" walk the dog and started to think of this "chore" as a chance to be out of the house and on to the trail. And so it was; walking the dog became part of my morning routine. We walked for an hour on the Trans Canada Trail every morning after I dropped the kids off at school. The trail was magnificent! It was well maintained through marshland, hilly terrain, and man-made staircases and walking bridges. I started to bring my camera and discovered the joy of nature photography. It was the same trail I had been walking on for years, and yet it was like seeing it for the first time — up close — EVERY day.

As for my daily walking routine, I am just shy of sixty-one years old, and I still walk at least five days a week; I take more pictures than ever, and I embrace all the magnificence that is along the way. I realize now how walking with my dog in nature rejuvenated my spirit and helped refresh my body and mind.

ASK QUESTIONS TO MAKE A CONNECTION

A lot of care and planning goes into matching a volunteer caregiver with a client. The caseworker responsible for matching caregiver and client accompanies the volunteer to the client's home or hospital room on their first visit. After formal introductions and a little sharing, the caseworker would make sure we had each other's contact information, decide on a visiting schedule, and make sure we had her cell number in case we had any questions. And then she was gone. This is the moment. You and a complete stranger "get to" know each other, face to face, both knowing that one of you has been told to get their affairs in order, and the other is there to help. Sometimes, a client might play "twenty questions" with me and want to know all about me; other times they would invite me to ask them questions. One time, a woman's first question for me was, "Would you attend my funeral?"

I remember Claire so clearly. She had beautiful long red hair. On one of my visits, she asked if I would help dye her hair. I told her I'd be happy to but that I had never dyed anyone's hair before. She laughed and said, "No pressure, but it had better turn out, because I won't have time to grow it out." As her cancer progressed, Claire was transferred to the hospital. One day when I was visiting her, she asked me to brush her hair. She sat up in her bed, and I brushed her hair softly and slowly, neither of us saying a word except and occasional "mmmm" from her. When she had had enough, she motioned me to stop. She gave me a big hug and whispered, "One day God will thank you for this," and without a thought, I whispered back, "He already has, Claire. He already has."

We never knew how long our relationship with our clients would be. For Claire, it was a few months. In the final days of her life, while I was visiting her in the hospital, she would mostly be sleeping. We had created a schedule with family and other volunteers so that she would have twenty-four-hour care and not die alone. I would sit by her bed and watch her sleep, sometimes wetting her lips with an ice cube when she would wake up with a cough, just momentarily. One time she woke up really confused and very afraid. She insisted that she needed to call her daughter. I was able to calm her a bit and dial the phone for her to hear her daughter's voice. Minutes later, she was asleep again. One time, I was holding her hand, she in her bed and me in a chair next to it. She fell asleep but didn't loosen her grip on my hand. We stayed that way a long time, and it was such a beautiful experience. I was totally with her, even though she was asleep.

I wasn't there when Claire died. I found out from the caseworker the following day. There was no funeral. The family decided against it. I was disappointed and resentful about their decision, because Claire had asked me, at our first meeting, if I would come to her funeral. I had said I would.

DON'T DOUBT WHAT YOU CAN GIVE

When I pulled up to Fran's address for the first time, I felt more nervous than I usually did at this initial visit. I knew right away it was because of the enormity and beauty of the house. It took up an entire corner lot. My self-talk kicked in, and I wondered if I was the right volunteer for Fran; would I be smart enough, would my manners be up to par, would I have anything interesting to talk to her about ... was I dressed okay?

Then my self-care training kicked in, and I remembered to close my eyes and take three deep breaths, deeply and slowly, focusing on my breath — breathe in, breathe out — 1, breathe in, breathe out, 2, breathe in, breathe out, 3... With my eyes still closed, I scanned my body and repeated in my head, *I am here, I am ready, I am at your service.*

In a much better frame of mind, I walked up to the door and rang the bell. Fran's husband opened the door, introduced himself as John, and invited me inside. He took my coat and led me to the sitting room to meet Fran. She was sitting in a wheelchair with a blanket on her lap, looking about as nervous as I was. John introduced us, offered me a seat, and then announced that he was off to the kitchen to make us tea. Here was that "moment" again: two strangers in a room, face to face for the first time, both knowing that one has been told to get their affairs in order and the other is there to help.

I jumped right in and commented on their beautiful home, asking Fran how long they had lived there. I could see her eyes start to tear up. She quickly pulled herself together, dabbed her eyes lightly with a tissue, and responded, "Twenty years. We built this house and raised our family here."

Thankfully, she asked me the next question, because I was feeling awkward and like I was making matters worse. She simply asked, "Tell me about yourself." While I was thinking of something interesting to say, she quickly added, "Do you have kids?"

And ... we were off!

We spent the first while drinking tea and talking about our kids, hers twenty-eight and thirty-two, mine four and seven. Fran was sixty-two and had short, straight white hair. She had retired from her career in nursing ten years ago; her husband had retired just the year before. At some point Fran asked me if I'd like to see the rest of the house. Would I? My house was littered with Lego blocks, packsacks, and primary school artwork. You knew as soon as you opened the door that kids lived there, but Fran's house was like a mansion to me. She showed me how to unlock the brakes on her wheelchair and then told me which way to go. It was the first time I had ever pushed someone in a wheelchair inside a house. I was nervous about scratching a table or knocking something over. Fran wasn't the chatty type, but she didn't seem to mind me inquiring about a photograph or a piece of art. The window coverings, the wallpaper, the antiques; I could see a lot of thought and love went into making this house their home. By the time we got back to the sitting room where we had begun, John was there putting our dishes onto a tray. He asked how we were getting on and Fran spoke first, asking me, "Would you like to come again?"

I remember feeling grateful on my drive home that day that Fran had chosen to continue with our match. First meetings are not always successful. It's a vulnerable and sensitive time. I felt like I had passed the first test.

I didn't see Fran again for two weeks because she had surgery on her back to relieve the pressure caused by a cancerous tumour. To my surprise, she was up and walking with a cane at my next visit. She reported feeling elated and optimistic for recovery, or at least a period of remission. With a little help, she could make it upstairs now and sleep in her own bed again beside her husband. This time while I was visiting, I sat on the end of her bed and we sorted through a box of photographs, Fran telling me who was in the picture, or the story that went with it, or what pile to put it in.

Time flew by, and before we knew it, John was knocking on the bedroom door to announce the nurse had arrived. That was my cue to wrap up, tidy up, and say goodbye until next week.

READ FAVOURITE BOOKS

A few weeks later, when I arrived one afternoon for my scheduled visit, Fran had had a setback. She was now walking on her own but was losing the feeling in her arms and hands. The tumour was pressing on the nerves at the base of her head and neck.

I helped her get into a comfortable position with pillows behind her back, behind her head, and under her arms. She looked exhausted. She asked me if I would read to her. I said, "Of course, I read to my kids all the time." She pointed to a thick hardcover book by C.S. Lewis on her shelf. I told her I was used to reading the likes of *The Cat in the Hat* and *Berenstain Bears* and warned her not to get too excited about my oratorical skills. She closed her eyes and assured me I would do just fine. I didn't get very far before she was asleep. I sat quietly watching her for a while. She breathed softly; I noticed she was thinner, and her skin was pale. She looked very peaceful.

Fran's health continued to deteriorate. Sometimes, when I arrived for my scheduled visit she would be sleeping, and John would slip out to run errands or have coffee with a friend. He was ever so grateful. I knew that without me there watching over Fran, he would not leave her side. One day, when I arrived for my visit, I learned that Fran was having trouble sleeping in her bed and having a lot of pain. The health-care team had ordered a hospital bed that was being delivered to the house that afternoon. I went upstairs to see how Fran was doing, and I could tell she was in pain. She always seemed delighted to see me. I smiled and gave her a hug and without asking pulled the book from the shelf ... now, where were we? Every now and then Fran would gently correct a word that I had pronounced incorrectly. If she saw the quizzical look on my face, she would define the word or expression. Sometimes I'd think she was asleep and stop reading. If she wasn't, she'd tell me softly, "Keep going." Other times, she would stop me and say, "Enough dear — I'm tired."

ALLOW INDEPENDENCE WHEN YOU CAN

The day her bed was being delivered, I made the mistake of saying, "Oh Fran, you must be excited to be getting your new bed; now you'll be able to get a good night's rest." As soon as the words left my mouth, we locked eyes in silence, and I realized this wasn't really good news. It meant that Fran was one step closer to the end. I immediately told her I was sorry for being insensitive, and she smiled and told me it was okay. "If I could use my arms, I'd give you a hug." I've never forgotten how that made me feel, and it happened over fifteen years ago.

Fran had a hospital table too, and a glass of water on it with a straw. When she wanted a drink, she would have to shimmy and struggle her head, neck, and shoulders to reach her mouth to the straw. It took everything I had not to help her up or pass her the water, but I knew by now that she cherished the small bits of independence she had left. I also knew that if she needed help, she would ask for it. I tried hard to pretend I wasn't noticing her struggles and continued reading. Fran was sleeping more now, and our reading sessions were getting shorter.

Then one day I got the call. Fran had passed peacefully in her sleep.

A few years later, while shopping at Chapters, my ten-year-old brought a book over to me and asked if we could get it. It was *The Lion, the Witch and the Wardrobe* by C.S. Lewis. I thought of my time with Fran and smiled. My heart was full. All those years later, these are still the "feeling" memories that are so easy to recall compared with dates and details.

CREATE MEANINGFUL PROJECTS

When I first met Eileen, I wouldn't even have guessed that she was sick. She insisted on making tea and served it up with slices of chocolate chip banana bread. The reason I remember that is because I asked her for the recipe. I still make it regularly all these years later...

Eileen had beaten cancer twenty years before, and it had returned with a vengeance. She was seventy-two and had decided not to go through with the aggressive treatment suggested by her medical team. It wouldn't have given her much more time, she said. She was given weeks to live, a month at most.

Her husband Andrew refused to leave her alone, and Eileen couldn't convince him that she would be fine for a few hours. Eileen knew she didn't have much time, and there was a lot to do. She reached out to the local palliative care association for help, and I was assigned to be her caregiver. Andrew stayed with us for the entire first meeting, even though Eileen assured him we would be fine. Afterward, he walked me to my car, shook my hand, looked at me, and said, "I don't know how I can thank you enough."

I replied, "Let me help you, Andrew."

On my next visit, Andrew was prepared with a list of errands he wanted to get done while I visited with Eileen. Once he was sure we were both comfortably sitting in the living room with our tea and lap blankets, he excused himself and was off. Eileen let out a very audible sigh, our eyes connected, and we broke into laughter. She told me she had her own list of things she wanted to get done, and not all of them included Andrew. Then she pointed to a cardboard box in the corner and asked me to put it on the coffee table and open it. There were piles of loose photos, homemade cards, letters and an assortment of ... mementos — I guessed.

When Eileen appeared with two brand new scrapbooks still in the cellophane, I said, "Ah, you have a project, I see." We got straight to work going through the box. We made two piles, one for each of their children. They had both been living in Southern Ontario for many years, raising their families. They had all been home for Thanksgiving just a few weeks before when Eileen had told them the news. Since then, they had been driving home on weekends to share in the last moments of her life.

Eileen knew she likely wouldn't have time to complete this project, but she could sort the things she had been saving since the kids were little. She found another box and divided everything up, marking their names on the boxes.

Andrew called to make sure everything was okay and let us know he would be home in about an hour. I made more tea while Eileen sorted through the boxes. Every now and then, she would come across something that prompted her to share a story or a memory. She read the Mother's Day cards out loud, showed me their graduation pictures, and then came the grandkids.

We were laughing our way through the family photo albums when Andrew returned. He had run into a friend after getting his hair cut, and they went for a beer. He looked like a new man.

They told me I wouldn't be needed the following week because their daughter was coming home. I didn't know it then, but that would be the last time I saw Eileen. She passed away in her sleep a few days after her daughter had arrived.

I went to her funeral to pay my respects but didn't stay long. It was really comforting for me to actually meet her kids, Charlene and Jordan, in person.

CARE FOR OTHER CAREGIVERS

A few weeks later, I got a call from Andrew, asking if I would visit him. The kids had gone home, and he was feeling lonely and out of sorts. We had tea and talked about Eileen. I suggested we take a walk in the bush and have a fire. Their property backed onto the bush, and I had seen snowmobile trails on my drive there. It was February, and Andrew hadn't been out for weeks except to run errands and get groceries. He was seventy-four but in good shape. We searched through three closets to find the right boots, his parka, gloves, and fur hat. We were ready. The sun was shining, and the snow crunched under our feet. Andrew had never just walked out back and had a fire in all the years he had lived in their house. In fact, he was a little skeptical about us being able to make one at all. I made sure I had matches and stuffed a few wieners in my pocket. Eventually, we found the right spot and set up camp. I cleared away an area; Andrew sat on a log and I looked for firewood. My kids had learned about winter survival at school, and I volunteered to accompany them during polar bear week, so I had learned too. It wasn't long before I had a fire going. Andrew was impressed, and he hadn't even seen the wieners yet! Roasting wieners is fun, even if you don't normally eat hot dogs. There's just something about roasting them on a stick over a fire that makes them irresistible. We sat in silence, roasting our wieners, staring into the fire. It was one of those magical, memorable moments; another one in the life of a caregiver.

I have so many beautiful and amazing memories of being a caregiver — so many moments of incredible support and gifts that went with end of life care, but from all of these experiences, what has become most clear to me is that what care recipients need most from caregivers is their full presence. But in order to give your full presence, you need to truly take care of yourself on all levels, mentally, emotionally, physically, and spiritually. Whether you use the strategies I described in this chapter or others that work for you, I encourage you to take time for yourself and access support when you need it.

CHAPTER NINE

SUPPORTING END-OF-LIFE CARE

CAROLE TESSIER

Carole Tessier works as a consultant psychiatrist in a variety of communities across Northern Ontario and Abitibi-Timiskaming, Quebec, and is an Assistant Professor with the Northern Ontario School of Medicine. She emphasizes the concept of acceptance and shares how she helped a patient with end of life care.

People often pray or offer life compromises in hopes of getting a certain wish or outcome in life. An example is the parent who prays or offers a life full of sacrifices to save the life of their sick child, or even going further and negotiating their own life in exchange for their terminally ill child to be saved. When my three-year-old daughter was diagnosed with leukemia, I cried, I prayed, I begged, I negotiated, and I was ready to give anything for her to live. We may be so afraid or want things so desperately that we have a difficult time seeing the bigger picture. Another example is the person who prays to be loved by someone specific or who has difficulty accepting the end of a relationship. This reminds me of a Garth Brooks song titled "Unanswered Prayers" in which he tells the story about seeing an old high school flame, the girl he thought was The One, and how he had prayed to be with her. In the end, he thanked God for the gifts he had in his life and realized these gifts may not have been possible if his prayers had been answered. It speaks to how we can wish for something but later realize that there was another experience in store for us and we end up being thankful that our prayers weren't answered.

Accepting happiness, or whatever is best for us and those around us, is not always what we think we want in the moment. It is about accepting some things are out of our control. Although I still wish my daughter and my family didn't have to go through these difficult few years, I have since been able to reflect on the growth we experienced both as individuals and as a family through our difficult ordeal with cancer.

Although I have come across many situations that make it difficult for me to believe events are merely coincidences in life, I can also respect the point of view of those who think the opposite and say nothing happens for a specific reason. It is a view and belief I have also held at certain times in my life, but when all is said and done, I now believe that perspective is everything. I often say, "whatever works," which is a view I have maintained throughout my professional life in my career, first as a midwife, then later as a medical student and physician, and now in my current work as a psychiatrist.

Specifically, I often tell myself *"whatever works"* when it comes to things people believe in, or things they do to make themselves feel better. If it relieves their emotional and/or physical pain, as long as it is not harmful or self-destructive, then it's worth a shot.

I have adopted this thinking to encompass and embrace alternative medicines or treatment modalities, whether I personally believe in them or not. It isn't for me to decide what can or will make my patients feel better. We are all individuals, and it makes sense that the same solution or treatment will likely not be successful for everyone. This also reminds me of a quote I heard in medical school that I have always remembered: "Medicine is the art of entertaining the patient while nature takes care of the problem." Although I certainly do not think this is always the case, it does speak to the reality that sometimes as physicians we do things to help our patients, but in the end, they may get better because of other reasons and not necessarily because of the treatment we offered them. It also speaks to the fact that sometimes there is nothing we can do to help a patient, and that is something any practitioner or caregiver needs to accept.

ACCEPT WHAT CAN'T BE CHANGED

Acceptance is a subject I often incorporate in my appointments with patients. Although I try to empower by guiding change in harmful behaviours, unhelpful ways of thinking, or even the problematic situations they find themselves in, there are always things that simply cannot be changed. For example, patients often have to accept that they can't change their past, whether it is a difficult childhood, parental neglect, or past abuse. The truth is no person has the power to change another. When it comes to acceptance, an important concept is often to accept that we don't have all the answers and likely never will. This applies to the earlier notion of finding a reason, an answer to the question "why," or whether events are purely coincidences. I accept that this is something I will never really know, and I certainly have had my share of "coincidences" in my personal life. That said, a story stands out as one that was difficult to ignore in these possible "life coincidences."

Mrs. Ray was a very special lady, the kind of person you immediately like in the first few minutes of meeting her. We first met in one of the northern out-of-town clinics I work at every few months, where I was asked to see her because she didn't have a family physician and wanted to discuss the possibility of Medical Assistance in Dying (MAID). Coincidently, or not, I was actually booked to attend training on Medical Assistance in Dying the following week. It was a hot topic in the medical field, since the province in which I work had recently passed legislation and MAID was now permitted. I wanted to be better informed and learn more about this sensitive topic, so I registered for the training, having no idea I was going to be needing this information so soon in order to help a patient.

Mrs. Ray had been diagnosed with Multiple System Atrophy (MSA) about three months before we met. Her health had been deteriorating for a few years, and she had been treated for what health-care providers thought was Parkinson's disease. I was not very familiar with MSA, but I looked it up and found that it is a term that brings together a group of neurodegenerative syndromes and is often misdiagnosed as Parkinson's disease. Management of MSA is what we call symptomatic because there are no effective disease-modifying treatments. In other words, there are no drugs to stop progression of the disease, and there is no cure. The time from the onset of MSA to disability varies but eventually leads to the need for a walking aid, then wheelchair confinement, then a bedridden state, and eventually death. The bottom line is that it is a devastating disease with no known cure.

INCORPORATE HUMOUR

I remember the first time Mrs. Ray walked into my office — specifically, I was struck by her sense of humour. When I questioned her about her day-to-day activities, she jokingly told me she'd been studying neurology in her spare time. When I asked her about substance use, she laughed and said "I try to take as much as possible," which was certainly not the case for her. She quickly clarified that she never used drugs in her life but had started taking medical cannabis in the past month. She told me the cannabis was helping her relax and sleep better at night. She added with a big grin that before the cannabis she "slept like a baby — waking up every three hours!"

GIVE CONTROL TO YOUR CARE RECIPIENT

Mrs. Ray explained that she felt relieved when she started looking into Medical Assistance in Dying, because she wanted the option of making her own decisions and having some control in the process of her deterioration and ultimately her death. She also said she felt lucky because she could have had something worse in terms of medical illness, and she felt good about the possibility of donating her body to science. It was remarkable to me that she was still able to see her situation in this positive light, despite the fact that she was deteriorating rapidly. Specifically, her speech had deteriorated significantly in the last six months, and she had great difficulty articulating words. She told me she was having difficulty walking and had to use a wheelchair and walker at home. She would lose her balance and frequently fall. She had a bilateral tremor, problems with constipation, and she had also started having problems with incontinence. Her energy level was low, and she was always tired. She had difficulty swallowing and had lost weight. Her appetite was good, but she had to cut her food in very small pieces and was mostly trying to eat soft foods like yogurt to prevent choking. She knew she would need a feeding tube in the near future and eventually would not be able to speak. She told me that her intention was to refuse a feeding tube, because she knew her situation would result in death either way, and she felt a tube would just prolong her situation.

She did not want her family to have to come and see her on a regular basis at the hospital for months on end, and she definitely did not want to be a burden on them. For now, she was living in an apartment in her daughter's home and receiving home care services once a week to help her take a shower safely. Despite her dire situation, she said she wasn't having any thoughts of suicide and told me she would not want to do that to her loved ones and definitely would not want them to find her like that. She did, however, say that suicide was something she would consider if she was refused access to Medical Assistance in Dying.

LET YOUR CARE RECIPIENT CONTROL THE TIMING

Mrs. Ray told me she had been thinking about Medical Assistance in Dying for the past year, and when she got the official diagnosis of MSA, she decided it was really something she wanted to do. She explained that she was not afraid of dying, since she knew her situation would not get better. She also said that if there were nothing in the afterlife, it would still be better than what was coming in terms of losing her independence.

After our first appointment, I concluded that there was no evidence to suggest any mood disorder or any other psychiatric disorders at the time, and in my medical professional opinion, she was capable of making her own decisions and was of sound mind. I told her at the time that I would try to assist her in finding resources for Medical Assistance in Dying when she felt the time was appropriate. I also told her that I was going for training on this very topic the following week and would be able to provide her with more information after that.

At the end of our first appointment, after walking Mrs. Ray and her daughter out of my office, I noticed her struggling to turn around and come back in to my office. She came toward me and asked if she could give me a hug. I automatically hugged her, without hesitation and without giving it any thought. That is something I have rarely done in my career as a physician, since we are taught the importance of maintaining professional boundaries with our patients. Admittedly, it was something that was much more common during my career as a midwife, where extending a hug at the end of a woman's labour and delivery or at the end of their care at the six-week postpartum mark was very normal. As midwives, we usually got to know our clients quite well over the course of their pregnancy, which is usually a very emotional time in their lives. In Mrs. Ray's case, I remember her daughter being surprised that her mother had come back to hug me, and she laughed as she told me, "You must be a really special person. My mom rarely ever gives hugs."

After she left, I couldn't help but reflect on the coincidence of meeting this patient a week before the MAID training session I was scheduled to attend. I felt compelled to help her in some way, but I wasn't exactly sure how I would be able to, since I didn't know if I would ever be able to personally administer medications to help a patient die. I had helped many people come into the world, but helping them leave was a whole other story. All I knew was that I needed to help her in some way, and that might be by helping her get answers, to find other health-care providers to help her in her journey, or possibly to assist her myself as a physician in her end-of-life procedure.

During the MAID training I attended, it became clear that Mrs. Ray was an appropriate candidate for MAID according to the established criteria.

Specifically, she had a grievous and irremediable medical condition that was serious and incurable and causing her significant disability. She was in an advanced state of irreversible decline and capability and was enduring suffering of a physical and psychological nature due to her illness, disability, and state of decline, which was intolerable to her and could not be relieved in a manner she considered acceptable.

After the training, I decided I was willing to assist Mrs. Ray in her end of life and would be one of the two required medical professionals to formally assess her ability to qualify for MAID and to participate in the actual procedure if needed. In some ways, and for multiple reasons, I was a bit nervous about the possibility of administering the medications myself, but I knew that if I were in a similar situation, I would want to have the option to be able to access MAID for myself or for a suffering loved one.

KEEP ALL FAMILY MEMBERS INFORMED

I met with Mrs. Ray in follow up several times after that. She was usually accompanied by one or two of her children, and on one occasion I went to see her at home, since it was increasingly difficult for her to get out. I shared with her and her family the information I had learned through the training session but also through speaking to a few health-care providers who had already participated in the MAID procedure. I was reassured by these other health-care providers that they had very special and positive experiences and that the patients and families had been very appreciative.

In terms of a date for the MAID procedure, Mrs. Ray decided to spend one last Christmas with her family and to try to wait a few more months after that for a specific and important event. Every time I met with her, she was deteriorating and reiterated her desire to proceed with MAID, and every time I met with her, I reminded her that she could always change her mind right up to the very last second, no matter what.

Another physician who was involved in her care was also willing to help with her request for medical assistance in dying. He agreed to be one of the official medical assessors and to administer the medications to her during the procedure.

Mrs. Ray chose a date to proceed with MAID. Plans were made for a home-care nurse to insert the IVs the day before the procedure, and I was amused to hear that the patient had told the nurse to come back the next morning instead, since she had decided to organize "a final party" the night before her death. A group of approximately forty people had gathered to reminisce and spend the last moments of her life with her. They had watched home videos and looked at family pictures. It was happy and sad. No one likes goodbyes, but as far as goodbyes go, I imagined it being as good as it gets.

On the day of the procedure, when I arrived at her home in the afternoon as planned, I was surprised to see how many people were reunited there with her. All five of her children and nine grandchildren were present, as well as the two family dogs. Mrs. Ray was sitting at her kitchen table surrounded by multiple family members, some of whom were having a glass of wine or beer. I couldn't help but smile when I noticed the glass of beer in front of her, which she sipped through a straw. Most of her family members around the table were laughing, smiling and chatting, although I noticed some of them had been crying and had tears in their eyes. Mrs. Ray was well-dressed, and her hair looked nice. She smiled at me and told me she was happy I was there. I told her I heard she had a party the night before and that I was happy for her. Upon questioning, Mrs. Ray still wanted to proceed with the MAID procedure.

The house got increasingly quiet as the other physician, the nurses, and I prepared the medication and documentation for the procedure. When the medications were ready, her son helped her into the living room, where a cozy fuzzy blanket was waiting for her on a comfortable recliner chair. Her son lifted her onto the chair, and she was ready. We obtained her consent again and explained the procedure to her family members, who were all gathered in the living room with a nice fire in the wood-burning fireplace. I told her it wouldn't be long and that she would go to her happy place; she answered with a smile and said she couldn't wait. Many of the family members were crying, and it was difficult for me to fight back tears as they took turns giving their last hugs and saying their last goodbyes, especially given the patient was also crying at this point. She still wanted to go through with it and appeared very calm and relaxed. Once the relaxant Midazolam was administered, she yawned and with a slurred speech and her usual bright smile told us it was a "wonderful drug." Those where her last words as she faded away.

Mrs. Ray was very appreciative of everyone involved in her end-of-life care and gladly agreed for me to share her story, whether it be to others in a similar situation, for teaching purposes, or in any other way that might be of benefit. With a mix of different emotions, including relief, sadness, and happiness, I decided to write about her story on my way back home that night. I wanted to write everything down in order to remember all the details and also to help me process this unique experience. Although I had a chance to debrief with the other health-care providers after the procedure, I believe writing Mrs. Ray's story was also my own way to debrief this very emotionally charged experience. Then, as "coincidence" would have it, I was asked to write this chapter and was given the opportunity to share this story on a much broader scale.

On the night of Mrs. Ray's passing, my father, who is a retired bus driver, was driving me on the long trip back home. I am very fortunate that he frequently accompanies me and drives me to and from my out-of-town work trips. Luckily, my father's reflexes and defensive driving skills kicked in that night as we found ourselves face-to-face with a transport truck that was coming toward us in our lane. The truck was passing another transport in a curve in the road, but my father was able to slow us down just enough for the transport to finish UN-safely passing and to move back into his lane at the very last second. I thanked my father for his good driving skills but also couldn't help wondering if there was a new angel watching over me that night. I silently looked up at the sky and thanked Mrs. Ray.

When I got home that night, I went to see my two daughters who were sleeping in their bedrooms and quietly kissed them. With tears rolling down my cheeks, I was filled with a variety of emotions. I felt thankful for my family, for having two beautiful, healthy daughters in my life, for my own health, and for being home safely. I also felt thankful to have been able to be a part of Mrs. Ray's journey and that I was able to help her leave the world on her own terms. As difficult as it is to explain, I felt I had now been involved in all cycles of life for my patients. From the beginning of the cycle of life, by welcoming newborn babies into this world, to now the end of the life cycle ... all the while being surrounded by emotional and grateful family members.

* * *

As I sit back and reflect on my role in Mrs. Ray's life and death, I feel more open to the idea that whether by coincidence or by purpose, sometimes in my role as a caregiver I just have to accept that I cannot fix things, and the best I can do is support someone on their journey, whether it be at the beginning, at the end, or somewhere in between. Some days are harder than others, but I always try to remember to be grateful for being where I am meant to be and for helping people as best as I can. And for the times I struggle, I like to remember the quote that says, "Sometimes the best thing you can do is not think, not wonder, not imagine, not obsess. Just breathe and have faith that everything will work out for the best."

CHAPTER TEN

A SPECIAL KIND OF CARE

LYNNE GOLDING

Lynne Golding is a lawyer and the author of a fiction series, "Beneath the Alders," novels that are loosely fictionalized reconstructions of Jessie Current's life in Brampton, Ontario, at the turn of the twentieth century. Here she tells of her caregiving journey with an elderly relative and what it taught her about independence.

When my Great-Aunt Jessie turned one hundred, I asked her if she would be willing to leave her long-term care home in Toronto and move into a brand-new long-term care home, ten minutes from my house and fifteen minutes from the neighbourhood in which she had been born and raised. When she agreed, I silently vowed that I would visit her once a week for the remaining years of her life. I confess, I didn't think there would be that many. But Jessie lived to be 108. Over those eight years, I learned a lot about Jessie's life growing up in Brampton and about her adult life elsewhere. I also learned a lot about caring for a loved one living in a long-term care home. Here are some of those lessons.

SUGGEST A HAPPY PILL

Getting Jessie to agree to move close to me turned out to be the easiest part of the process. Once she agreed to relocate, I had to make it happen. This involved working with two different Community Care Access Centres, the governmental organizations then responsible for arranging the placement of those requiring nursing home care in Ontario. Since Jessie was leaving one geographical area and entering another, I had to deal with two. That was no easy task. Eventually, I delivered completed paperwork for both CCACs, and she was authorized to move.

The home Jessie was leaving was older. It was filled with her own furniture — well-loved pieces she had lived with for decades. The room she was moving into was slightly smaller and contained standard-issue furniture. Little of it could come with her. She had to sort, select, and discard. I packed what was left, found and retained professional movers, and oversaw the placement of boxes and furniture into and out of the truck. Under Jessie's direction, I hung her pictures and unpacked her things, placing her Moorcroft pottery and her many books where she desired them. That evening, the rest of my family arrived to welcome her to her new home and to sup with her in the home's family dining room. I left that night exhausted but exhilarated with the pleasure I was sure I had brought to my dear aunt.

That feeling of accomplishment, of having done a good turn, the saintly glow that emanated from my very being, lasted for about six weeks. I had just mailed the final address change forms for her bank accounts and miscellaneous bills when Jessie began to complain. The person who resided in the room above hers dragged furniture across the floor in the middle of the night. The staff served food and cleared dishes from the wrong side of her. She did not like her tablemates. She wanted to return to Toronto. I was crestfallen — hurt that she would rather be in a home she had come to dislike with few if no visitors than be near me in this new home. I was also overwhelmed at the thought of completing the moving process in reverse.

As I wrestled with what to do, Jessie's poor temper was noticed by one of her good friends. Elaine wrote a letter to the home saying that Jessie was not doing the things she normally loved to do: she was no longer listening to the CBC; no longer watching baseball; no longer painting watercolours. Elaine did not attribute this altered behaviour to the place Jessie was living. She thought Jessie was depressed.

The home summoned a geriatric psychologist who tested Jessie and diagnosed her with mild depression. Her brain, it seems, had ceased to produce a sufficient quantity of dopamine. She was prescribed a half pill a day of a mild antidepressant, a pill we came to know as "Jessie's happy pill." It was one of only two pills she took each day.

Jessie never resumed listening to the radio or watching baseball, but she began to participate in the home's activities. She became happy in the new room to which she was relocated, this one on the top floor of the home. My angelic glow returned. I was once again the good niece.

DON'T TREAT SENIORS LIKE CHILDREN

Although Jessie needed the assistance of a walker or, more often, a wheelchair in her ambulation, for the most part this did not stop her from getting out and about. On nice days, I would push Jessie's wheelchair near the home's gardens or through the surrounding neighbourhood, where we could admire flowers in various states of bloom. For two gals who hailed from Brampton —once the "Flowertown of Canada" — we marvelled at how few flowers we could identify by name. Jessie at least had the excuse of the onset of dementia. My mother-in-law pushed her down a four-lane near-highway to get to McDonalds, one of Jessie's favourite restaurants.

But her excursions were not limited to those to which she could be pushed. With assistance getting in and out of cars, Jessie was able to go farther afield. (Put the walker or wheelchair as close as possible to the open door; assist her to standing; place a hand on the top of the door; turn her back to the seat and have her sit down; lift her legs into the car as her body twisted forward; put the device in the trunk.) In this way, Jessie was able to attend appointments, go to the mall, and the museum, and dine with my parents at Red Lobster (another one of her favourites) or at my house. In time, that in and out of the car routine became too onerous, and we switched to booking wheelchair taxis. (Roll her up, strap her in, and off she goes.)

My practice in using these taxis was to order them a day ahead of time for a specified hour. I would ask the staff at the home to have Jessie ready for pickup — coat and hat donned —ten minutes before the desired hour of our departure. I would arrive at the same time in order to accompany her to our destination.

The arrangements worked well — generally like clockwork. One day, however, it seemed that everyone's clock was set too fast — everyone's but mine. On that day, I arrived at the home, surprised that Jessie was not waiting at the front door. Surprise turned to alarm when I could not find her anywhere in the home. Alarm turned to panic when I was told that on that day, the taxi arrived half an hour early, and since Jessie was fully prepared, she was loaded into the taxi and driven away. "You sent her on her own?" I asked incredulously. "With a stranger?"

I began to imagine what could have befallen her. She could be in a ditch, her wallet emptied of its few dollars. She could be halfway to the border, a senior-knapping ransom note being readied. Or more likely, and only slightly less distressingly, she could have been unceremoniously dropped off at the front door of the restaurant, left alone, scared, and confused.

The staff at the home called the restaurant and then handed me the phone. I was told that Jessie had been brought inside the restaurant by the taxi driver and was at that time sitting by herself at the table reserved for our family, watching fish swim in a wall-sized aquarium, quite happy with the change of scenery.

I was reminded of a few things. First of all, a senior is not a child. Jessie did not need my physical presence to be taken in a taxi. Second, I needed to deliver much clearer instructions to the staff of the home if I did not want Jessie to be sent off without me. Third, I needed to have far more trust in those wheelchair taxi drivers!

IF YOU DON'T USE IT, YOU LOSE IT

In December of Jessie's 101st year, we established a new tradition. It had been years since she had decorated any room for Christmas. I made a trip to Winners and purchased a few select pieces. That year and every year for the next seven, I would hold up a decoration and she would tell me where in the room it should be placed: a wreath on the door; a velvet-clad, long-bearded Father Christmas on her cedar chest; a very miniature Christmas tree on her bedside table.

Then we would go down to the home's communal kitchen, make some tea, and write out her Christmas cards. I would bring preaddressed labels, a box of cards, and a pen. She would address the inside of each card, write a few lines, and sign her name. Then I would place the card in the envelope and seal and stamp it. In the case of her six young great-nieces and nephews, I would include a cheque in an amount she determined appropriate. I had long ago assumed responsibility for writing cheques on her behalf.

Though the number of card recipients decreased each year with the passing of others younger than her, the time it took to write the cards increased. It was harder and harder for Jessie to hold a pen. The writing process took longer and longer. One year, I thought it would be easier for her if she dictated to me the contents of the cards. She would simply sign them. The next year, wanting to further ease her efforts, I signed them for her too. Unfortunately, the cards she signed the year before were the last things she ever signed; the last words she ever wrote. I later came to realize that in attempting to ease her burdens, I had deprived her of one of her last physical abilities. I should have been more patient and allowed her to spend ten minutes on a card. After all, what more did she have to do?

REMOVE SMALL VALUABLES, BUT ONLY ONCE THEY CEASE TO PROVIDE PLEASURE

Jessie was married for only fifteen of her 108 years. But the fervid romance—beginning in her late forties—that preceded her near elopement endured throughout her marriage. The couple's devotion to one other was captured in a number of ways, including in a lengthy correspondence, the fruits of which were stored in a big, hard-sided, turquoise suitcase. Those letters, frequently extracted and reread, kept Warren with Jessie in the forty years after he left this world. As Jessie moved from home to large apartment, to smaller apartment, to a large retirement home room, to smaller and smaller nursing home rooms, her keepsakes of Warren were reduced to three: the big suitcase of letters; a large 24" by 36" wall-mounted black-and-white framed photo (Warren looking sporty in casual golf attire) and her platinum, diamond wedding ring.

When Jessie moved into the new home, we were advised that valuable items, particularly small items like jewellery, should be stored elsewhere. Jessie, who lived a frugal life, had only one valuable piece of jewellery: her wedding ring. Removing it from her hand while she still derived any pleasure from wearing it was out of the question. For as long as she could associate it with Warren, she would rather wear it and take a chance on losing it than remove it to a place of safety for a later beneficiary of her estate.

Although Jessie's memory was very good when she moved into the home at the age of one hundred, as the years went on she began to live further back in her memory. She could not recall what she ate for breakfast any day I visited her, but she could vividly recall what she ate for breakfast most mornings as a child. At one point she said to me, "Who is that man on the wall?"

"Jessie," I said, "that's your husband, Warren." In retrospect, that was when I should have suggested that I take the ring to a safety deposit box. But it did not occur to me that she might have been ready to remove it from her crooked, arthritic ring finger.

From the two-paned casement window in Jessie's room, she had a full view of the neighbourhood to the south, the cars driving along the road on their way to and from that neighbourhood, and of those coming and going from the home. Near the window was Jessie's old seven-drawer mahogany desk. It had been years since she had written anything at it, but it served as a useful piece of furniture to hold her large convex-screened, deeper-than-wide television. Facing toward the desk and the television was her bed. The placement of the furniture made getting to the window in a wheelchair not impossible, but a bit tricky.

One day, when Jessie was 105, she wheeled her chair to the desk, used it as support to stand, and then began walking. Jessie had not been able to walk unaided in years. She was no more able to do so on that day. In seconds, she crashed to the floor. She was found by one of the staff members shortly afterward, her hip broken, her wedding ring gone.

Why did she try to walk that day? What was it she sought to do? Was she trying to get to the window, to see the houses across the way—the houses that were frequently compared (unfavourably) to those built by her grandfather? I can't see why. Did she wish to see the clouds in the blue sky, which had in former years been the subject of so much interest to her sister and had now become an interest of hers? I hope she didn't break her hip to see those. I like to think that she stood to retrieve her ring; that it had fallen to the floor and rolled toward the window; or that it had been left the night before on the far side of the desk. She was never able to recall the reason for her impetuous activity. She was never able to recall when she had last seen the ring.

Jessie came home from the hospital some time later with a new hip installed. Though her room had been combed by many staff members and family, the ring was never found. The lesson: to avoid loss, remove precious small items from the room of your loved one, but do it exactly the moment before they cease to bring the pleasure they were meant to bestow. I cannot tell you how to identify that moment.

REPORT BAD (AND GOOD) BEHAVIOUR

Jessie fell in the home two hundred times! No, not really, but that is what she told us. Every time a visitor asked her how she was after the day she broke her hip, she replied mournfully that she had fallen earlier that day. After repeated assurances from staff that no such fall had occurred, and seeing no bandages, casts or other indicia of broken bones, we soon responded to such declarations in the kind but dismissive way one would upon hearing that a sock could not be found.

Jessie's time in the hospital following the break of her hip was not her only time there. Every time a urinary tract infection got out of control, an ambulance would be called. Fever-ridden, Jessie would have a distressing ride to the hospital to obtain the antibiotics that could not be administered in the home. Once there, she would lie on a gurney in a hallway, sometimes for six to eighteen hours, before being admitted to a room where she would stay for five days or so until the infection was eliminated. Then she would return to her home in another ambulance, always with less acuity than when she left.

One day when I went to see Jessie in the home, I noticed dark black marks on her arms. Her skin at that time was paper-thin. It could tear with the slightest strain, turn dark purple with bruising at the slightest knock. But these marks on her arms were large, hand-sized. "Jessie," I said, "how did you get those marks?" She named the staff member. I knew the name. Jessie had complained about the worker before. "Maybe your skin is very sensitive today?" No, Jessie said. The worker was hard. I knew there was no reason to handle a resident hard. The home had a machine that gently lifted patients from bed to chair, to toilet, or to bath.

That worker was not on shift at that time. I spoke to another staff member about it. How did she think the bruises were caused? She would not look me in the eye when she denied any knowledge. I asked whether the particular worker had been on shift that day or—for good measure—the day before. I was told the worker was.

Then I struggled. What was I to do with that information? The accusation came from a woman who mistakenly believed that she fell every day. How reliable was this accusation? Perhaps the bruises had been caused in some other way. Perhaps the worker took hold of Jessie to prevent her from falling while bathing. I didn't want to ruin the worker's career. But I wanted to protect my aunt and others in the home in the event the accusations were true.

In the end, I reported the alleged incident to the executive director of the home. Her immediate reaction was to cite Jessie's increasingly confused state. I conceded that but insisted that the matter be recorded in Jessie's file and as an unconfirmed allegation in the file of the worker—just in case the family members of other residents made similar reports. Some months later, the executive director called me to tell me that another allegation had been made against that worker. The worker would no longer be employed at the home. The police were involved. Asking for the matter to be recorded —even marked as being unsubstantiated — had been the right thing to do.

GO WITH THE FLOW

I was not Jessie's only visitor. She was blessed with many family members and friends, all of them of another generation, of course. It was a great comfort to me to know that other people visited Jessie during the week, since my visits were usually confined to weekends.

One weekday afternoon, I found myself unexpectedly in the vicinity of Jessie's home. I decided to drop by for a short visit. I wasn't surprised to see the lobby area of the home filled with residents in wheelchairs. Residents were frequently moved to that location to be entertained. There is no shortage of gifted musicians ready to volunteer their time to perform for the residents or to lead them in sing-alongs. On this day, there was no music. The man before them wore white vestments. He held in one hand a chalice and in the other a wafer. As he blessed those assembled, I spotted Jessie sitting on the end of a row of wheelchairs. I found a straight-backed chair and pulled it beside her.

The priest began making his way to each resident, offering the holy elements. When he got to Jessie, I caught his eye. "Father," I said, raising my hand, glad that I had arrived before any sacrilege had occurred. "Jessie is Protestant."

"My dear," he replied. "Jessie has been taking Catholic communion with us once a month for the past five years." I lowered my hand and urged him to carry on. I tried not to think about what her father would have said.

LETTING GO AT THE END

Jessie contracted her last urinary tract infection while my husband and I were away in Switzerland. I received a call from the home telling me that she had been sent to the hospital again, delirious with a high fever. We flew home as soon as we could. I arrived at the hospital the next day to find her in the emergency room area, accompanied by my mother-in-law. She would be admitted to a room shortly and have to stay there for at least four or five days while the antibiotics did their miraculous work and while she was rehydrated.

Jessie was conscious of my presence that day and the next. She seemed to understand what I was saying to her as I prattled away about the things I had seen in Europe. But she wasn't the same. I turned my mind to the Do Not Resuscitate order she had executed years earlier. She was 108. She had no short-term and not much long-term memory. She couldn't walk. She could barely talk. Even before the latest infection, eating had become a struggle. She was being infused with saline solution and antibiotics. At what point were the measures being taken the heroic ones she did not want? How would I know?

I was saved from having to answer that question by Jessie herself. Later that night, I received a call from the hospital. The intravenous needle had fallen out of Jessie's thin, tired veins. The nurses were trying to reinsert it, but her vein had collapsed and they were having difficulty finding a new one. Eventually, Jessie told them to stop. "It's enough," she said. The next morning, I confirmed her instructions. She did not want any further intravenous injections of drugs or any sustenance. She wanted to go home.

She left the hospital the following day, returning to her second floor room, to be tended to by the staff she had come to love. My brother and sister-in-law and I sat with her the next few days and evenings as other family members and friends came to bid their final farewells. She never said another word. She only opened her eyes one more time.

It was a Friday morning. I was alone with Jessie. For the first time in days, I opened the curtains in her room, exposing it to the bright February day. Around ten in the morning, she gave my hand a squeeze. I looked up to see her eyes open. She was staring at the ceiling. I followed her gaze. A bright ray of light was bouncing off the ceiling where it met the wall in front of her. She never took her eyes off it. *What does she see*, I wondered? Then it occurred to me. She saw them all: her mother, her father, her grandfather, her sister, Ina, her brother, Jim, her dear niece, Laura, and, of course, her husband, Warren. "They've come for you, Jessie," I whispered, continuing to hold her hand. "You can go to them." And she did. It was at once the saddest and most beautiful moment I had ever experienced.

CHAPTER ELEVEN

RECORDING LIFE, EVEN AS IT IS ENDING

KIMBERLEY RIVANDO-ROBB

As a personal support worker, Kimberley Rivando-Robb discovered that no matter the task at hand — hair combing, clothing, feeding — what really mattered was that her clients had a chance to recount and record their story. The other end of dignity is being allowed to remember that you lived and it mattered.

Growing up, I loved listening to the stories of people around me — the personal histories of what made them who they were and why they did the things they did. How did they end up exactly here at this exact point in time? I wanted to know.

In grade three, my class was given the opportunity to sit and read to the elderly folks at a local long-term care facility. We were matched with an elderly person, and every week we would meet and read to them. Most of the kids saw it as a chore and dutifully read to their partner. They hated it. But I loved it. I was matched with a quirky older lady who wore cat's-eye glasses and swore like a sailor. Although I'm sure she enjoyed me reading to her, she had a habit of cutting me off and telling me stories of her life with great detail and description. I would sit for the whole hour, unmoving, just trying to soak up the stories of her life. I listened carefully and watched as she animatedly told me about past lovers, past regrets, her family, where she grew up, and her opinion on almost everything. It was amazing and far beyond what a typical child of that age should have been listening to. I didn't care where or how I got the book; I just needed the story.

I still remember the crushing feeling in my heart when I ran from the bus into the lobby of the long-term care home and couldn't find my reading partner sitting amongst the crowd. I was taken aside and told that she had passed away peacefully in her sleep. I was sad that she was gone, but I was also incredibly disappointed that she had passed away peacefully. I wanted her death to be more. I wanted her to die in some crazy adventure. My childlike mind imagined her fighting a pirate, stealing someone's lunch, and swinging away from the nursing home on a tree limb; I don't know. Just something that fit her style. That was what stuck with me most — that her story ended quietly simply wasn't her!

Following my heart, I obtained my English Language and Literature degree and had great plans to be a writer. I had high hopes of writing my generation's most loved and sought-after books, but I quickly realized the difficulty in that and decided to get my post-graduate degree in journalism instead. My new plan was to travel across the world to war-torn countries and write the truth about their oppression. I wanted to tell the stories of those living there, the truth that we often don't get to hear, the truth that is toned down for our sensitive ears and the truth that is buried. I was a young woman on a mission, not to be dissuaded from my choices. I was determined to make a difference in the world.

At twenty-six, I went through a difficult breakup and hit my rock bottom. My life coming up to that point was filled with difficult moments and too many shut doors. My heartbreaking experiences had built up to the point where I felt myself struggling to keep my head above water, so to speak. I was still helping those around me to find their path, to find their journey through listening to their stories, and I was good at it. I definitely had the art of listening and storytelling down pat, but I didn't consider it something that I wanted to do; more something that just came naturally. I could sit for endless hours and listen to friends' issues. I heard the incline in their voices and knew what excited them. I could also hear the declines and knew what part of their story that needed an adjustment. It may sound strange, but as they spoke, I could see the words being written in my mind, and listening in that way made it easier to hear beyond the actual words that were being spoken. I could "see" what they were saying and also what they were not saying. I didn't know it at the time, but I was listening from a different place — an intuitive place. It was as though I could slow it down enough to hear not only through my ears and my mind, but I could also hear it in my gut and then respond with advice from my own deep place of inner knowing. It was something I came to realize that people were needing and craving —someone to just sit and listen deeply without judgement as they told the difficult parts of their story and the meaning they'd attached to it.

After many long walks, crying sessions, days spent in bed, feeling as though I was going nowhere in life, my dad and stepmother suggested that I get my Personal Support Worker diploma just for something to do (other than moping around). My dad knew that I loved caring for people and had an interest in the medical field with a keen ability to see beyond illness and pain. At first I hated the idea; why would I want to change bedpans? I had heard so much negativity surrounding the job and had heard many of my nursing friends vent about these glorified people who thought they were nurses but had no real credentials. Truthfully, I think that that's what made me sign up the very next day. I mean, how could anyone who was helping the sick be that bad? I wanted to prove my friends wrong about "bad" PSWs. So I signed up, took the course, and graduated at the top of my class.

One of the requirements for graduation was to complete more than 320 unpaid work hours in two separate placements. The first placement I completed was in a busy long-term care home. I hated it. I got to know the residents and grew to love them. I wanted to spend time washing their hair and listening as they told me stories of their childhoods; feeding them breakfast as they recounted their life struggles; tucking them into bed while hearing about their children and parents. But instead I was on a locked floor with patients with Alzheimer's disease and dementia. It was there that I first experienced the misconception that these patients had lost their minds: that they were no longer "people" because they didn't remember and couldn't function as "normal" people do. I was beyond angry at this logic. If anyone bothered to listen to these patients, they would quickly realize that they could tell their truth and remember much of what really happened in their lives, especially events that were emotionally charged, even if it was all wrapped up in a fictional story.

Due to everything being timed and the lack of staff, there was simply no time for us to spend time lovingly washing hair or listening. Patients were rushed and shuttled through their stations, usually to end up in front of the TV or around a dinner table to have food crammed in their mouths by exhausted and worn-out workers. It was horrible. I listened to a man at another table trying to tell his caregiver about the war and how the oatmeal reminded him of it, only to have another spoonful shoved into his mouth as the next person waited for their spoonful. It wasn't a good situation, and I felt as though I had made a giant mistake by becoming a PSW. Fortunately, my next placement was at a hospice, and that was where my whole perspective on caregiving changed. It was where I found my purpose.

TAKE THE EXTRA TIME

I had never feared death or those experiencing it. Granted, I hadn't been around many people walking the last moments of their journey, but it just never struck me as something to be feared. In my mind, it was a process that we would all go through at some point. I already had it in my mind that it was as much as part of life as breathing, love, and adventures. I'm not sure why or when I developed those ideas, but on my very first day, I realized that my beliefs about death made me a perfect fit for hospice work. To me, it was a magical place. It had pain, compassion, fear, love, family, hate, urgency, time to listen. It had every component of life and the stories that come from life.

The thing I noticed immediately was the amount of time I had to do my work and to connect with the dying person, as well as the family members who were present. That was not only encouraged but also expected. I had the opportunity to hear from the woman who had twelve kids and devoted her life to them. I got to hear from the man who travelled all around the world, only to discover that he wanted nothing more than to find a cottage up north and live in solitude. I got to give luxurious baths with scalp massages. I got to watch people sink into the warm water and let go of their anxiety and pain as their minds travelled with the stories I told.

SEARCH YOUR OWN SOUL

At that time, I was doing a lot of soul-searching myself. I wanted to understand what it meant to be dying. Not in a medical or physiological sense, but the deep internal process happening in the mind and in the soul. I wanted to understand why people feared death, and if that fear actually disappeared when it came closer to their last breath; when the body was just spent, and all that remained was the spirit and the life within. It was difficult for me because I was on the opposite side of life. I was, for the most part, very healthy compared with the people I was caring for. That made it hard to put myself into that mindset.

I must admit, I was in above my head and not quite sure how to ask the questions that I wanted answers to. The amazing thing, though, is that at the hospice we are encouraged to chat, to listen, to question, and to allow people to express themselves in their own way. People can sense when you're open and ready to listen, and I found that those who had something to say could sense I was ready and willing to listen. They loved to open up to me. And these were the magical moments. I was lucky enough to be hired on at first casually and later part-time after completing my placement and dove deeper into my personal research on caregiving and the end-of-life journey.

MAKE A PERSONAL CONNECTION

At this time I also accepted a position at a long-term care home, on the crisis floor, a temporary floor where patients with Alzheimer's disease and dementia and those who were entering into palliative care would stay for a brief period before moving on to a more permanent placement. When I accepted the position, I was excited and thought it would be a nice balance with working at the hospice, but I was in for a complete shock. Perhaps the home had the right idea when it first began, but somewhere along the line lost its drive and positive focus on patient care. On my floor, there were three separate large rooms with smaller bedrooms in each room. There were usually five patients per room with two PSWs caring for up to fifteen patients. There were baby monitors so we could hear if anything went wrong, but it was an awful system. We often found patients lying on the floor or having soiled themselves, but we would have no idea because we were tending to other patients and simply couldn't be everywhere at once. With everyone having high needs, it was very difficult to maintain the level of care we wanted to provide. Many residents spent their days sitting in a chair, staring at the wall.

There was one lady in particular, who I'll call Ethel, who really touched my heart. She had Lewy Body Dementia and was a "handful." She would bite, kick, scratch, and punch anyone who came near her, which made our job very difficult and something of a hazard. She wouldn't talk to anyone, she didn't connect with her family, and she lashed out at anyone who came close to her. After a particularly difficult shift where I had feces thrown at me and Ethel had punched me in the head, I sat at a stop sign and bawled my eyes out. It wasn't that I was hurt at all — I had played rugby for a long time, had taken all kinds of martial arts and had been a bouncer for a few years — I could take the physical aspects of my job. What made it hard was the fact that after every aggressive act, if I looked into Ethel's eyes, I could see pure panic and pain. It killed me that I couldn't do anything to help soothe the deeper parts of her that clearly needed to be taken care of. As I sat there at the stop sign, it dawned on me that maybe I could try to ease her pain using her past, her stories, and the memories she had lost.

The very next day, I called a few of her family members and tried to find out some information about who she was. I jotted down where she grew up, who her family was, where she worked, her favourite foods, and anything else that had to do with her life and who she was as a person. I wrote it all out on loose-leaf paper and then created a simple booklet that included some images from magazines to add to the descriptions. I knew that she couldn't read or remember anything written and that I might never be able to get close enough to show her the images, but I knew I needed to try something new. It was a long shot, but I hoped that somehow it would help ease her mind and give her some peace. So, on my next shift, at the very beginning of her day, I verbally gave her a run-down of her daily routine, interlaced with tidbits about her life to help remind her of who she was. I read it from cover to cover. Although she was still very restless, I did manage to capture and hold her attention the entire time.

At the end of my shift, it occurred to me that she hadn't caused physical harm to anyone. I thought it might be a coincidence, but in case it wasn't, I left the booklet with a sticky note asking anyone who came in to work to read it to her at the beginning of her day and as often as possible throughout the day. I didn't expect much and was shocked when I came back to work after a few days off to find her sitting with other people. Actually sitting, not smiling, but sitting, looking around and calmly letting the day go by! Apparently, she hadn't had any issues with violence. She had even smiled once or twice and had begun spending time with other residents. To this day, I'm not entirely sure why her book brought about a change, but I am convinced that it did have something to do with listening, reassuring, and respecting her need for comfort, familiarity, and understanding. I created a few more of those books during my time at the home, but sadly, felt I needed to leave my job when the state of the home began to negatively impact my own personal well-being.

UNDERSTAND THE FEAR OF BEING FORGOTTEN

I started spending more time working at the hospice and growing in my understanding of life and death. Speaking with a woman I knew in the community outside of the hospice, I dared to ask her what was causing her stress, why death was so frightening to her in her final walk of life. Naively, I thought it was death itself that people were afraid of. That it was the thought of being buried or of never seeing loved ones again, or of letting go of life. But she looked me right in the eye and said that she was ready to die. Her pain, both physical and mental, was at an all-time high. She could no longer do the things she used to do. She said she was ready to let go and move on to whatever waited for her after this life. She could see my confusion. If it wasn't what I thought was causing her all of this anxiety around dying, what was it?

She explained that what scared her most was the thought of being forgotten. Sure, people would remember the stories she had told them and would remember her stories from their perspective, but those weren't real. The emotions, the feelings, the adventures, the things she had experienced *were* real, and were what made her who she was. She told me about her daughter who would never know about her dancing on a bar to a Ricky Martin song or about the time she burned her bra in university. Her daughter was having a very hard time with her mother's imminent death and had shut down in some ways. She didn't want to spend as much time with her mother, since she felt it was awkward and just didn't know how to cope.

I decided to sit with this woman and jot down as many of her stories as I could. It was time-consuming, but I was determined to get her stories on paper. When we were finished, I printed off the rough draft and gave it to her. I wasn't sure if there were any limitations; I was just a random friend stopping by, so I told her that if she wanted to share them with her daughter she should definitely do so, but at her own discretion.

The next time I stopped by, I found out that she had given the pages to her daughter, and it had been received far better than either of us could have imagined. It had created the opening that they needed to reconnect. To laugh. To cry. To talk about things her daughter never would have had any idea about. It became a comfort blanket, so to speak, and she felt as though she was no longer taking her memories with her. Her legacy was no longer dying with her; instead, it had been memorialized on paper. I later found out that when she died, she was anxiety-free and happy simply to let go. I couldn't have asked for anything more, and I'm so honoured to have been able to help with that process.

CHERISH THE VALUE OF MEMORIES

The knowledge that people valued their memories and experiences so greatly allowed me to help people recall these stories and share them with their families. I quickly put into place a new business plan and started my own business focusing on the emotional and mental well-being of people in various states of being, from all walks of life, by creating memory and legacy books. I also find joy in teaching people how they can record and share their stories with their families on their own.

Fast-forward four years, and I'm still working at the hospice and working at my business. It can be very stressful at times, but for the most part I feel that as a caregiver I am able to let things go better than most. At the hospice, I am with people for a brief moment of their lives, and although we do connect and form bonds, our main purpose is to soothe, ease pain, show compassion, and hold space during the last walk of life. If we can take away even a brief amount of pain — mental, physical, emotional, or spiritual — we are doing our jobs and fulfilling our purpose.

And now, when I sit down to create a person's legacy or memory book, I know that I'm doing something that will help them to move through death just a little bit easier. I've also come to understand that everyone has a story to tell. Everyone wants to be remembered, thought of, and wants to share their experience, and there's no reason they shouldn't be able to!

RELEASE THE PAIN AND EMBRACE SELF-CARE

Both in my job at the hospice and with the legacy books that I create, I have on occasion gotten too close to a person and felt their death in a very intense way. I cope with that through meditation and by walking in the forest. On these walks, I talk out loud to the part of myself that is feeling pain, to the part that feels the loss, and I reflect on the things I did to make that person's life better. I think about their stories, and I am filled with the knowledge that they lived a life of their own making, with both positive and negative experiences, because that is what it truly means to live.

Knowing that the rate of burnout among caregivers is high when we neglect self-care, I have made it my mission to live my life to the beat of my own drum and in a way that suits me rather than that which suits others. When I'm feeling emotionally, physically, or mentally fragile, I venture out into the woods and use the power of the natural world to heal me. I meditate. I go inside. I listen to my inner voice and the healing voice of nature. One thing I know for sure is that being busy and constantly working isn't a sign of success, but instead a sure-fire way to take yourself out as a caregiver. My personal motto is that I can't help anyone if I am down and out. I can only be fully present and impactful when I am healthy and have the energy to give. For this to be possible, I have to pay attention to my nutrition, my spirituality, my health, my body... It's a full circle that must be nourished.

I believe that from the moment we are born, our life journey begins to write itself. Each year is a new addition to the book, each month a new chapter, each day a new line. We must be brave enough to create and live out our own stories, not those that are dictated to us. The ups and downs, adventures and perils, from heartbreaks to weddings, victories and defeats, deaths, births, and all the life-changing moments, these are the stories that make up our lives, the stories that deserve to be told, remembered, celebrated, and treasured. Every person living on Earth has a unique story, having travelled down different paths and experiencing events that no other person will encounter in the same way. There is something simply amazing about seeing your life in print, having something that you can pass down through the generations. If we look back through the decades, from the beginning of time, humans have used rock, paper, verbal stories, and books to record their lives, and I genuinely believe it is an art that must be continued.

Now, when I sit down to create a person's legacy or memory book, I know that I'm doing something that will help them to move through death just a little bit easier. I've also come to understand that everyone has a story to tell. Everyone wants to be remembered, thought of, and wants to share their experience, and there's no reason they shouldn't be able to!

CHAPTER TWELVE

HOW TO NOURISH YOUR BODY

THERESA ALBERT

Theresa Albert is a nutritionist who has counselled countless clients in the simple ways to nourish on the go. Her biggest caregiving role so far has been as a working mom, where she discovered a knack for high-nutrient, low-effort food. Her recipes below are built for comfort *and* speed.

P rofessionally, I have taken care of countless clients in private practice as a nutritionist, endless friends and loved ones after accidents, deaths, surgeries, divorces, and miscellaneous disasters. But I will be the first to admit that am not good at the touchy-feely side of life that requires the patience and calm of caregiving. My impulse is to do something practical that can be crossed off a list. The more scientific edge of my profession soothes that need in me: input nutrient A into problem B and watch for solution. Even stress has a nutritional resolution; simply increase intake of B-complex Vitamins; 100 mg per day usually during the midday slump.

My longest-running caregiving role so far was one that blindsided me, even though it was a state that most women desire, crave, and plan for: pregnancy. I was a reluctant mom, since it was unexpected, so I was highly anxious that the maternal instinct would not kick in as it "should." To me, being trained in food means that even my chef head says nurturing is delivered on a spoon and not much else. I like exact measurements and methods that can deliver specific results.

Parenting my perfectly normal and healthy single child came with the usual minor bumps and bruises, but so far on this twenty-three-year journey, no major setbacks. I have developed some mothering/nurturing skills along the way that have helped me slow down and listen rather than take action, but it isn't my first tool. I am a caregiver who has had to find another way to care. No matter how empty and tired I feel at the end of the day, the sensory experience of washing vegetables, the sound of chopping them, and the sizzle in a pan as the smell wafts to my nose is a comfort. It took me a long time to understand that most people feel the opposite. When the strain and relentlessness of caregiving sets in, most people would prefer to do just about anything other than cook.

DON'T RESIST COOKING — EVERYONE LOVES A GOOD MEAL

All the other diapering, entertaining, mind-reading part of being a parent was extremely slow and painful for me. On top of that, the guilt that I felt for not being "that kind of mom" was immense, until I figured out that I loved doing the thing that the other mothers detested. The excessively caring and kind women at the "mommy and me" Fridays took my shaking, unsure mess of a self and showed me how to manage by laughing, taking breaks, joining book clubs, and the like. I observed their skills in disciplining, encouraging, teaching their kids and parroted what seemed to work for me and my kid. I sat in on the classes teaching ASL to enhance baby communication prelanguage with hand signals; I did all the *things*. But when I looked around the room at the maternity-leave moms who were going back to their careers in law, art curation, opera, accounting ... I learned that the one skill I had that terrified/tired them was preparing meals. Man, they overwhelmingly hated it!

I believe that food is our greatest comfort, only source of energy, and a critical part of what brings a family together. It has traditionally brought a community together around the fire pit, common baking ovens, or celebrations. And yet somehow in our culture it has become just another task to tick off the list and/or get out of. And that is when life is going smoothly, this task goes on the back burner when the demands of caregiving kick up.

I learned that the weight of feeding the group often falls more heavily upon the caregiver. To me, food is the way that the earth communicates with every cell in the body, and I take pleasure in being able to focus on it. And yet when there is extra strain on your time, energy, and stress level, it is often the first thing to go.

REMEMBER, FOOD AND STRESS DON'T GET ALONG

When the body is under stress, either when you are caregiver or care recipient, the hunger signals are all out of whack. The fight-or-flight hormone cortisol is designed to shut down the any requirement to stop, and that includes eating. The body prioritizes the flight from danger. The problem is that this may be danger you can't run from, and it could be prolonged. Some people overeat mindlessly, and there is some anthropological evidence that chewing (what would have been greens, leaves or herbs, not high-calorie chips and popcorn) keeps the mind alert and engages the parasympathetic nervous system to soothe. Many people in this heightened nervous state lose their appetite since the gut is filled with more neurons than the brain, and they are all firing out of sync. The temptation is to skip meals, grab from a vending machine, or munch from a drive-through. Of course, this can make matters worse.

Layer on the fact that hospitals, doctors' offices, and on-the-go options are rarely nourishing in any way, but they do fill the hole. There is finally evidence that points to these types of low-nutrient foods as being linked to increased risk of cancer. The sad fact is that it is common for the caregiver to become sick as a result of the strain, and what multiplies that concern is poor diet. As for the patient, most if not all medications are nutrient-depleting, so the demand for high-nutrient food is even greater. And who doesn't feel improved, even for just a minute, during and after a good meal?

STOCK UP ON EASY, DELICIOUS, NOURISHING RECIPES

Having a handful of nourishing, simple recipes can make life easy, no matter what kind of hiccups are in your day. I've gathered a few of the lifesavers that I have used for myself on a busy week to deliver to a friend who is running from pillar to post after a loved one falls, has an accident, needs surgery, or is just having that kind of day. Each takes merely a few minutes to pull together and delivers nutrient density. Nutrient density is particularly critical for children and the elderly, whose appetite or meal opportunities may be lacking, but the imperative is even greater on a caregiving journey. During these stressful times, every spoonful counts and must be filled with high-nutrient fuel, because you simply don't know if you will get another spoonful in, or when.

START YOUR DAY WITH A TURBO POWER RECIPE

MAGIC MUESLI

This is an amazing bowlful of turbo-power super foods that can start any day, provide a quick snack, and even travel with you. It can be mixed ahead and sit in the fridge for 4–5 days. In a pinch, I have stuffed it into an ice cream cone and eaten it in the car. Scale up as needed so you always have a bowl in the fridge.

Preparation time: 6 minutes
Servings: 2

½ cup plain, full-fat yogurt
1 apple, grated or ½ cup unsweetened applesauce
1 tbsp uncooked oatmeal
1 tbsp slivered almonds
1 tbsp chia seeds
½ cup frozen blueberries
¼ cup hulled hemp seeds
1 tsp ground cinnamon
1 tsp turmeric

Mix all of the ingredients together and you will have the right amount of protein (about 10 grams), fibre, and nutrients to set you up for the day. Serve immediately or cover and keep in fridge up to 5 days.

SAVE STEPS BY DOUBLE-BATCHING

THREE-WAY RECIPE: MEATLOAF/BALLS/BURGERS

From the same couple pounds of ground beef or chicken, you can have three meals ready to go! It is the same basic mixture to make meatloaf, meatballs, and burgers, so why not save all three in the freezer for those go to days? Or just make three meatloaves at once; the possibilities are varied and the dinners are on the table fast. Chia seeds act as a binding agent and are a fabulous fibre hidden in an otherwise unsuspecting meal.

Preparation Time: Half an hour
Serving Size: 12

> 1 cup seasoned breadcrumbs
> ¼ cup chia seeds
> 1 tsp onion powder
> 1 tsp garlic powder
> 1 tsp dried thyme
> 1 egg
> 2 tsp Worcestershire sauce
> 1/4 cup ketchup
> 1/2 cup unsweetened applesauce
> salt and pepper
> 2 pounds extra lean ground beef (preferably organic)

In a large bowl, combine everything but the ground beef and mix well. Using a fork, mix in ground beef but do not compress, since it will toughen the meat.

1. Divide mixture into thirds and place one third into a loaf pan and lightly pat down. Cover with foil and freeze.
2. Using the second third, make 4 burger patties and lay on a plate lined with foil. Freeze until solid enough to move without sticking together and place into a freezer bag.
3. Roll remaining into small balls and freeze as you did the burgers.

TO COOK:

Meatloaf: In oven at 400°F for 1.5 to 2 hours. Uncover at about the halfway point and insert meat thermometer. Be sure that internal temperature reaches 185°F or 85°C.

Burgers: Can be pan-fried directly from frozen, check temperature as above.

Meatballs: Bake in 400°F oven from frozen uncovered and on a baking sheet for about 30–45 minutes. Check temperature as above. Stir into a pot with your favourite tomato sauce just to warm through. Serve over pasta or on hot dog buns for a meatball sandwich.

PREPARE THE BEST AND SIMPLEST COMFORT FOOD

BAKED MASHED POTATOES WITH BONUS POTATO SKINS
This is the simplest recipe for the planet's best comfort food ... and since you bake rather than peel and boil, you retain all of the nutrients as well as get a second meal out of it. The skins are saved and double-baked to create potato skins with cheese.

Preparation Time: 15 minutes
Serving size: 6

> 6 medium baking potatoes
> 1/2 cup plain Greek yogurt
> 2 tsp butter
> 1 tsp garlic powder
> 1 tbsp dried rosemary
> 1–3 cups grated cheddar cheese
> 1 cup salsa

Preheat oven to 450°F.

Scrub baking potatoes with a brush. Prick with a fork in several places and place potatoes in oven and bake for 45 minutes to 1 hour.

When they are soft, allow to cool or hold with a clean towel and cut in half, scoop insides into a large bowl, and add yogurt, butter, and garlic powder. Mash with potato masher and mix until they are the consistency that you like. Serve as is.

BAKED POTATO SKINS
Store skins in the fridge in a single layer in a container, and when ready for a quick snack, lay the potato skins out onto a baking sheet and sprinkle with garlic powder, salt, and dried rosemary. Top with cheese and bake at 425°F just to melt cheese.

NOTE: These can be made ahead and frozen or refrigerated, so keep this recipe in mind any time you have the oven on for an hour or so, bake some potatoes.

FEED A CROWD OR YOURSELF WITH THIS EASY-PREP, NUTRIENT-RICH RECIPE

RED LENTIL AND SWEET POTATO SOUP

Preparation Time: 25 minutes
Serving size: 8–10

You can feed a family of eight for under $4.00 with a soup of high-protein lentils, nutrition-packed sweet potatoes, and onions. This recipe avoids all of the common allergens, feeds vegans, vegetarians, and is a crowd pleaser even for carnivores. It has become a go to soup to deliver to a household in need.

> 1 tsp butter
> 1 onion, chopped
> 2 cups dry red lentils
> 2 small sweet potatoes, cubed
> 4 cups chicken or vegetable broth
> 4 cups water
> 1 tbsp dried basil
> ½ tsp black pepper
> 2 tsp dried red chili peppers
> 1 tsp turmeric
> 2 tbsp molasses
> 8 tbsp grated cheddar cheese (optional)

Warm a large pot over medium-high heat and melt butter. Add onions and sweet potatoes; stir. Add broth and water; add lentils. Bring to a boil, turn down to simmer, and cover. Let simmer for 20 minutes. Stir in basil, chili peppers, pepper, turmeric, and molasses. Serve topped with cheese.

KNOW WHEN ALL YOU WANT IS A SOOTHING BEVERAGE

GOLDEN COCONUT LATTE

This recipe not only packs a powerful nutrient punch — it is also a soothing beverage both for the caregiver and the recipient. Feel free to substitute cow's milk if it is well tolerated, but the coconut milk does provide some of the medium chain triglycerides that are heart-protective and anti-inflammatory.

Preparation Time: 2 minutes
Servings: 2

> 3 cups coconut milk (unsweetened)
> 1-inch piece fresh ginger, grated
> 1 tbsp ground turmeric
> 1 tbsp ground cinnamon
> 1 tbsp honey

Mix ingredients together in a large measuring cup. Warm in microwave for 3 minutes and let stand to steep for 2–4 minutes. Pour into a mug or glass through a strainer (or let the solids sink to the bottom and drink around them in a pinch)

DRINK COMFORTING ANTI-OX COCOA

Hot cocoa reminds us all of cozy days, but the store-bought stuff is loaded with fillers and sugar ... the worst thing for your health. You know that chocolate is good for you, but dark chocolate cocoa powder is the best because it has no sugar and is loaded with antioxidants.

Preparation Time: 2 minutes
Servings: 1

    1 tsp cocoa powder
    2 tsp maple syrup
    6 oz boiling water
    2 oz milk or alternative
    1/4 tsp cinnamon

Whisk together the cocoa powder with the maple syrup for 2–3 minutes until completely mixed into a paste. Add boiling water, whisking continuously. Top with milk. Sprinkle with cinnamon.

SOOTHE YOURSELF INTO SLUMBER WITH A HIGH-MAGNESIUM RECIPE

SLEEP-NUT COOKIES

Magnesium is the nutrient that muscles need to relax, and when you are tense, you need even more of it. One way is to soak in Epsom salts, which is simply magnesium absorbed through the skin; another is to take a supplement before bed, and a third is to increase the magnesium-containing foods that will help your body deal with the tense and still muscles. Here is an evening snack to be eaten two or three hours before bed that will increase your magnesium level in the tastiest way possible and soothe you into slumber. Two cookies and one cup of milk is an excellent high-magnesium snack that contains less than 300 calories.

Preparation time: 10 minutes
Servings: 36 cookies (2 cookies per serving)

> 2 cups any combo of all-natural peanut butter and/or almond butter/ any nut butter
> ¼ cup molasses
> ¼ cup honey
> 1 large egg
> 3–6 tbsp whole-wheat flour or alternative (amount depends upon the grind of the nuts)

Combine all ingredients except flour in a bowl and mix with a spatula. Sprinkle in 1 tbsp flour at a time until dough comes together and is quite thick and less sticky. Use your hands to roll into 36 small balls and place onto a baking sheet. Press with a fork. Bake at 350°F for 8–10 minutes. The cookies should be a little soft in the middle; they will harden as they cool.

* * *

Any way you slice it, both the caregiver and the one in need of care will need to eat a few times each day, and it may be low on your list. If I have learned anything, it is that everyone is soothed by a good meal, whether they can make it or not, can eat it or not. It is still a tried and true way to show you care, even if it is just for this minute and just for yourself.

CHAPTER THIRTEEN

MITIGATING THE COSTS OF CARING

CAROLINE TAPP-MACDOUGALL

As the founder of Canada Cares, an organization dedicated to raising awareness of the work of Caregivers and Development Manager of Canadian Abilities Foundation, Caroline Tapp-MacDougall has heard and lived countless stories and learned some key things. The financial side of caregiving isn't something we want to think about (who thinks about money when life hangs in the balance?), but it is a common apex of stress.

When my father, Ralph, was diagnosed with Amyotrophic Lateral Sclerosis (also known as ALS, Lou Gehrig's disease, or motor neuron disease), life changed. He died within three years, leaving my mother with no savings and an outstanding mortgage, which she struggled to pay with her very small pensions and RSP withdrawals. A few years later, she had a debilitating stroke and needed twenty-four-hour care. I was responsible, whether I liked it or not.

Since ALS is a disease that paralyzes people, Dad's ability to cope with financial matters was short-lived. Faster than normal, his brain was no longer able to communicate with the muscles of his body. As his muscles broke down, he became depressed, lost his ability to walk, talk, eat, swallow, and eventually breathe. Mum had never balanced a budget, written a cheque, or handled weekly or monthly bills. She did not understand how credit card interest worked. In the stressful aftermath of Dad's death, Mom ran up $20,000 worth of debt within six months (without saying or paying anything).

I was forty-five and had three young children and a business to run. My parents lived a traffic-filled ninety-minute drive from my home in the city and had been fiercely private and independent about money. It was simply not discussed. I hadn't realized the dire financial straits that they were in until Dad could no longer handle the day-to-day challenges of robbing Peter to pay Paul and juggling the bills.

GET AN ACCURATE FINANCIAL ASSESSMENT

When family members or friends become frail or ill, the care we need to provide often extends to assisting with financial decision-making. In some cases, there are dependents, spouses, and family members to take into consideration. Perhaps there are assets and investment portfolios to manage, rental properties and tenants to take care of. Is there a family home to sell or rent and additional cars, SUVs, boats, bikes, vacation properties/

timeshares, and businesses affairs to deal with? In others, there are debts, promissory notes, legal matters, and "money messes" that seem to stretch far and wide.

Whether you and your loved one have been penny-wise and pound-foolish, frugal, extravagant, or somewhere in between, there are critical financial matters that a family caregiver must sort out right away. A delay will impact not only your ability to provide good care and pay the "medical bills" (yes there will be some even in Canada with our amazing universal health-care system), but the impending chaos of ignoring things will place undue stress on you and other family members down the road.

Getting an accurate assessment of the situation is key.

ASK FOR PERSONAL AND FINANCIAL PAPERWORK

You'll need to track down lots of official and unofficial documents, online passwords, and authorizations to have access to accounts and records that you'll need to "do your job" over the coming months.

At this point, your concerns should be threefold:
1. Knowing what you need;
2. Knowing where to find it; and
3. Knowing or finding a reliable contact who is familiar with your family member's history with their organization.

Seek and ye shall find... For some people, all the documents/records will be nicely organized for you in matching file folders and in a safe place with copies stored at a lawyer's or trusted advisor's office. As a prudent person, I urge you to make sure yours are easy to access and all in one place. You just don't know when the tables will flip. Perhaps there's an online spot such as a Google Doc's where everything can be found at the push of a button. There may even be a secret Swiss bank account. However, if your parents or the person you'll be looking after is anything like my parents, you'll be on a hunting expedition through drawers, file folders, emails, and shoeboxes in an effort to make sense of both "the big picture" and the day-to-day details.

Here's a beginners list of things you'll need to ask about or look for

KNOW WHERE TO FIND...

If you're lucky enough to have all these documents organized for you, keep them in a safe place. Hint: It's wise to give advisors copies as well. Here's what you need for a no-surprise approach.

- Banking information (often there's more than one bank)
- Loan records (to whom and how much)
- Copies of leases or rental agreements (car, condo, apartment, appliances, furnace, hot water tank)
- Government health information (provincial health card)
- Insurance policies (health, life)
- Investments (RRSP, stocks etc.) — statements and original certificates
- Pension information — government and private
- Mortgage on home and cottage/investment properties
- Wills/power of attorney for property and personal care
- Commitments for charitable donations (regular and upon death)
- Birth certificate
- Social insurance number
- Passport
- Veterans Affairs
- Club memberships or subscriptions
- Relatives' addresses and phone numbers

DRILL DOWN TO THE DETAILS

I started my story by saying that there are two things I believe all caregivers should do. The first is to be open and vulnerable with your loved one about your emotions and how you are handling the situation. Being open and transparent may provide your loved one with a safe place that will allow him or her to feel comfortable to share with you. Even if it's just admitting to your care recipient that you don't know whether you should act normal or that you don't know what to talk about now that the typical day-to-day stuff seems so superficial and irrelevant. Perhaps your care recipient will say that they want to pretend nothing is wrong, or maybe they will use the opening to talk about what's really going on inside of them.

Some financial matters are recurring, while others are annual or are based on renewals. You'll want to:

Review automatic deposits such as pensions (CPP, employment-related or private pensions, both from local and overseas sources), plus royalties, rent from tenants occupying income properties, loan repayments, and, of course, interest.

On the flip side, you'll likely find conveniently set up **automatic withdrawals** to cover cell phones, car payments, utilities, mortgages, insurance premiums, loan repayments, etc. A word of caution: sometimes these amounts are set up to be charged to a credit card instead of from a bank account. Track them down.

You'll also need to check and see if there are outstanding loans or **credit card debts**. Ideally, you can find the credit cards in a purse or wallet and official paperwork. You need to figure how much is really owing, and repayment terms. Sometimes there are some nasty surprises in store here for family members who had no idea that credit cards had been run up, cottages remortgaged. You should check into the method of payment, interest rates, and repayment term. Watch for home equity loans, a newly popular but potentially risky financial instrument that a lot of seniors are using to convert home equity into funds to cover daily living and/or medical expenses.

When I was away one weekend, my mother signed a complicated contract with a door-to-door salesman to replace all of the windows in her house. The new energy-efficient triple-pane ones cost $15,000 plus installation. He convinced her to go ahead, even though she couldn't afford the purchase, by offering a buy now, pay later plan. Sadly, the windows were not only overpriced and poor quality, but some of her jewellery also went missing during the installation. Mum was clearly embarrassed when I found out. Not to mention we had to deal with sorting out the sixty-month installment plan, which went on long after the house, was sold.

- ✔ Dig up copies of leases or rental agreements for cars, condo, appliances, furnace, and hot water tank. Again, you'll want to understand the terms and conditions, liabilities, and opportunities for cancellation or renegotiation.
- ✔ Perhaps easier to find, your parent or loved one's provincial health card, SIN, or Social Security number, and any additional medical insurance cards for private or company plans that you'll need to show at the pharmacy, treatment centres, or official offices.

✔ Get a copy of all insurance policies (the fine print is important). Full life or term policies employee health-care policies, dental plans, and home and auto. Review the coverage. Is it all still necessary? How are premiums paid? What is covered?

✔ Check government benefits

✔ Everyone could use a little luck at times like this ... don't forget to look for and *check lottery tickets*. After all, with all your hard work and your loved one's changing needs, a little luck might be in order.

CHECK DETAILS OF HEALTH PLANS AND ALL INSURANCES

While it wasn't a great dental plan for a senior, my mother's Blue Cross dental plan actually covered the cost of her wheelchair and a decent portion of the private nursing care she needed. However, when he started to get sick, my father fought hard to maintain financial privacy, and in the process he got confused between home and auto automatic deductions. This meant that he forgot to notify the insurance company when he was no longer able to drive the car, paid for five months of wasted coverage, and, somehow, managed to cancel the home insurance premiums; luckily we caught it all and restored order.

REMEMBER THAT POWER OF ATTORNEY IS ESSENTIAL

To assume legal responsibility for the person's affairs, you will have to produce two documents, one for personal care and the other for property. These documents will need to be produced on all sorts of occasions, especially when you're role is new and transfer of money, payments, or signatures are required. Keep them handy.

TABULATE THE COST OF CARE

It's never too early to plan: Many of us are being introduced to the financial issues of growing older as we help our parents or siblings navigate their way through their housing and health care options.

In whatever situation, a wise financial plan should include consideration for the many changing and unknown situations that come with caregiving. Know that after years of saving, many seniors are reluctant to both accept help and/or spend money to cover their costs of care, even if they have it. You may need to be persuasive, or if you can, arrange quietly for services that are needed. It helps to pry the funds loose by bringing awareness to the fact that "this is why you worked and saved all your life ... this *is* the rainy day." Be aware that you have the option to pay privately for the services you need if you can afford them, and that is often a very good alternative to waiting in line or being left without the best care.

Getting prepared: Try to determine your level of preparedness by answering these eight important questions:

- Do you or your parents have a realistic budget that includes income and expenses?
- Is there enough flexibility to cover possible extras like medical care or alternate housing arrangements?
- Are they taking advantage of disability tax credits or government pensions or veterans affairs, if they qualify?
- The rules aren't always clear. Try to figure out what is covered by provincial health plans and private/company insurance and what will need to be paid for out of savings. Will you need a budget for transportation costs (Uber, taxi, assisted services, ambulance transfers)?
- Can flexibility and extra cash or ongoing income be realized by renting or selling properties?
- Explore the financial instruments and tools that are at your disposal with the bank or a trusted advisor. Might a reverse mortgage, cashing in an insurance policy, or a GIC make sense?
- Who, if anyone, will cover the costs of your time off work to provide care? (I've heard of families getting together and deciding to pay one sibling an official full- or part-time salary to take care of their parents and their needs). Investigate government assistance programs.

ASK TAX SERVICES QUESTIONS

You may be eligible for deductions:

- Payments to authorized medical practitioners such as physicians, dentists, or nurses for medical, dental, and other medical-related services.
- An air conditioner purchase of $1,000 or 50 percent of the amount paid, whichever is less, is an eligible medical expense. Normally, a person with a severe chronic ailment, disease, or disorder can make the claim, although a prescription is required.

- Dentures and dental implants can be claimed without any certification or prescription.
- The amount paid for an electric or sealed combustion furnace bought to replace a furnace that is neither of these, where the replacement is required because of a person's severe chronic respiratory ailment or immune system disorder, can be claimed. Again, you'll need a prescription to make this claim.
- Medical marijuana costs will be accepted when the substances are purchased in accordance with the "Access to Cannabis for Medical Purposes Regulations" or section 56 of the *Controlled Drugs and Substances Act*.

SAMPLE BUDGET

MONTHLY INCOME

Wages/Salary (You)	$ _____
Wages/Salary (Spouse)	$ _____
Investment Income	$ _____
Government Benefits	$ _____
TOTAL MONEY IN	$ _____

MONTHLY SAVINGS & INVESTMENTS

Savings	$ _____
RRSP	$ _____
Spousal RRSP	$ _____
Education Fund	$ _____
Pension Plan Contributions	$ _____
Tax-sheltered Non-registered Investments	$ _____
SUBTOTAL	$ _____

MONTHLY FIXED LIVING EXPENSES

Mortgage	$ _____
UTILITIES	
Heat	$ _____

Light $ _____
Telephone $ _____
Water $ _____
Cable/Satellite $ _____
Loan Payments $ _____
Car Lease $ _____
INSURANCE
Life $ _____
Disability $ _____
Critical Illness $ _____
Long-Term Care $ _____
Car $ _____
Household (Contents, Fire) $ _____
Child or Elder Care $ _____
Other $ _____
SUBTOTAL $ _____

VARIABLE MONTHLY LIVING EXPENSES
Transportation $ _____
Food $ _____
Clothing $ _____
Home Maintenance $ _____
Furnishings $ _____
Personal Care $ _____
Medical and Dental $ _____
Education/Self-Improvement $ _____
Vacations $ _____
Charitable Donations $ _____
Bank Charges/Fees $ _____
Miscellaneous $ _____
SUBTOTAL $ _____

TOTAL MONEY OUT $ _____

MONTHLY EXCESS OR LOSS $ _____

EXPECT THE UNEXPECTED

Expect change. Expect to be flexible and expect plenty of surprises along the way during your caregiving journey. At the end of the day, providing care, sharing in someone's most challenging times and assuming financial management tasks is very personal. Some of us have more disposable income to call on. Some of us have large and helpful families, others don't. Some costs are covered by our governments and private insurance plans, but many are not.

Simply put, every caregiving situation is different. How much time and money you are able to spend to maintain your quality of life is up to you ... but what I can tell you is that establishing an accurate financial picture and staying up to speed with ongoing expenses will make a significant difference in your ability to have and maintain a healthy caregiving experience.

SHARE YOUR STORY WITH US

We hope that these heartfelt stories have helped you through a time of transition. Please let us know, either by writing to us at the address below or emailing us at hello@bluemoonpublishers.com

If you have a story you'd like to share with us, for possible inclusion in our Insights books within the Wish I Knew series, please feel free to send those to us at submissions@bluemoonpublishers.com .

NEXT CHAPTER PRESS

We create books that help people through life's transitions.

We all face changes, transitions, and life-altering experiences during the story of our life. From milestones to tragedies, some chapters are joyful and exciting, while others are sad and challenging.

If you are turning a page in your life, we hope our books will be a source of comfort, strength and inspiration. Written by people who have been through what you're experiencing or have helped others along a similar path, our books will help you move forward with experiences shared, lessons learned, and wisdom gained.

Everyone's story is written with many chapters, and we hope our books accompany you during this next stage of your life and help make it as meaningful as possible.

NEXT CHAPTER PRESS

An Imprint of Blue Moon Publishers